T0158796

Jesus Laughing

The Laughing Christ

By

Reverend Ellen Wallace Douglas

www.trafford.com
North America & international
toll-free: 1 888 232 4444 (USA & Canada)
fax: 812 355 4082

Dedication

This book is dedicated to The Reverend Penny A. Donovan,D.D.,
for opening the door to my lighted path.

Table of Contents

Foreword

By Rev. Penny A. Donovan, D.D.

When one steps upon the spiritual path the first challenge that meets us is that of letting go of long held concepts of what and who we think Jesus the Christ might be. Whether we believe him to be the Son of God or just a very convincing speaker, prophet and teacher, doesn't detract from the fact that he is still the most fascinating and influential person in history. Two thousand years after his death he still brings to the human heart the proof of life eternal and love immortal. His teachings are as meaningful today as they were when he walked the earth. Jesus' words and deeds have altered minds, mended broken lives, and brought powerful men to their knees before a forgiving God. No one else before or since can make that claim.

Yet Jesus remains one of the most controversial of people, and even those who are not well acquainted with him still have strong opinions about him. There are as many interpretations about his teachings as there are people, and these interpretations come from the heart. And this is part of Jesus' charm; no one is neutral about his or her feelings concerning him.

Ellen Douglas is not neutral about her feelings for Jesus either. In this book you will find a treasure of new insights, and interesting interpretations of Jesus' words. Ellen presents to the reader an invitation to look deeper, think stronger, and open the mind to the wonders of his teachings. Presented from the heart, this book is sure to affect the reader in very positive ways. Read, learn, grow, and come to know a side of Jesus most people don't see.

PREFACE

Until one is committed, there is hesitancy, the chance to draw back, always ineffectiveness. Concerning all acts of initiative (and creation), there is one elementary truth, the ignorance of which kills countless ideas and splendid plans:

> That the moment one definitely commits oneself, then Providence moves too. All sorts of things occur to help one that would never otherwise have occurred. A whole stream of events issue from the decision, raising in one's favor all manner of unforeseen incidents and meetings and material assistance, which no one could have dreamt would have come his way.
>
> **W. H. Murray,**
> ***The Scottish Himalayan Expedition***

The idea for this book came to me on June 25, 1998 in meditation. As soon as I made the commitment to write it, Providence moved, too. A whole stream of events issued forth and indeed all manner of unforeseen incidents occurred to propel me toward the publication of this inspired work. One such event was the offer of another student of Springwell Metaphysical Studies to type this manuscript, in exchange for being the first to read it! The vastness of the task at times overwhelmed my imagination until I finally realized that this was a task I agreed to before birth into this particular incarnation. It is my fervent prayer that all who read it will learn of themselves as only the individual can; as a holy child of God, created from His Holy Essence: boundless love, unspeakable joy, profound peace and perfect harmony.

Originally I was going to title this book 'Metaphysical Jesus', but then one day I looked up and on my wall saw a picture which was given to me. Its title was 'The Laughing Christ' and it showed a picture of Master Jesus with an open-mouth laugh, as though he were truly joyous about life. I decided then to change the title.

Some of the books to which I will refer include The Aquarian Gospel of Jesus the Christ, written by Levi Dowling, a medical doctor and minister, when he was given the text from a Spirit entity. It is what is known as 'channeled' information. Other books include *A Course In Miracles*, channeled from Jesus through Helen Schucman; *The Life and Teachings of the Masters of the Far East*, by Baird T. Spalding; *The Other Bible*, edited by Willis Barnstone; and various editions of the Apocryphal books.

"The name 'Apocrypha' (from Greek) means 'hidden, concealed.' Originally the word seems to have been entirely appropriate, for it was given to such works as were prepared for certain sects or companies of heretical believers, who carefully concealed them from the public. The evidence of this fact is seen in some of the titles of these sacred books; for example, a papyrus of the first century has as its title, "*A Holy and Secret Book of Moses*, called the Eighth or Holy." The term "apocryphal" in its original sense was thus honorable, but later it came to specify books that were rejected.' *The Ancestry of Our English Bible*, p. 140

Conjectural phrases are found in the Introduction of *The Other Bible*: "Why did the specifically Jewish and Christian texts fail to find a place in the Bible? Was it a question of divine authority, period, doctrine? These errant scriptures are often aesthetically and religiously the equal of books in the canon and offer vital information such as infancy gospels on Jesus' childhood, as well as alternate versions of major biblical stories . . . Deprived of all scriptures between the Testaments, the common reader is left with the impression that somehow Christianity sprang self-generated like a divine entity, with no past, into its historical setting. Yet a reading of the texts between the Testaments shows how major eschatological themes of the New Testament – the appearance of the Son of Man, the imminence of the End, the apocalyptic vision in the Book of Revelation, the notion of salvation through the messiah – are all the preoccupation of intertestamental literature." pp. xviii-xix

The reason I felt a need to write this book is that my life changed as a result of learning the lessons taught by Archangel Gabriel, channeling through Rev. Penny A. Donovan, from October 25, 1987 through December 3, 1999. When he first came to teach us, he said that he would come for twelve years, and he did. Only a fraction of what he taught us is included here. The future will see many books written based on these teachings. We called them teachings, but Archangel Gabriel told us that he came only to remind us of what we *already know*. Everything Archangel Gabriel said is available in print and/or audiocassette tape. (See Bibliography.)

I have brought together writings and recordings extant about Jesus and what we have now come to know therefrom about the circumstances of his conception, birth, childhood and worldly travels, including his lessons in the temple in Egypt. Also, I describe the trial and crucifixion, the resurrection and the various materializations after his so-called 'death'. From this information we learn that through all his incarnations Jesus knew that he was a holy child of God, but he also knew that the human race had lost an awareness of that divine connection. As a child of God and given free choice, he decided to come and save the world, but only on the cross did he realize that he could not save anyone else; that salvation is an individual path which each one of us must take. Not with permission from another nor based on a special connection to another, not facilitated by another, but directly from the individual Self to the Creator God. We are all prodigals in this 'far country',[1] earth. We are all going back home to God.[2] By our own free choice each of us will determine just when that return will take place.

This is a story about Jesus the Christ, who was not the first Christ to come to earth,[3] but the last Christ to come to earth so that he, by his example,[4] could show us the way and thereby teach us what we must learn for our own salvation. It is time, indeed it is way past time to understand that Jesus the Christ came not to start a new religion[5], for he was a good Jew, but to ground forever the Light of Truth to the earth's sphere for all of humanity for all time to come. And from that Light we may benefit and consciously begin our path back home to God.[6]

We look to the eastern sky for the dawning of a new day. The early light brings to some a new hope, to some continuing pain, to others another challenge, to yet others a continuing joy. There is a broader horizon which humanity does not see with physical eyes – a new dawning which affects us profoundly. The universe we live in revolves around a Central Sun[7] and its segments are the zodiac. The age now coming to a close, Pisces, brought Jesus the Christ, who grounded the light of truth to earth forevermore for all humanity. Now the Age of Aquarius[8] dawns and all around us we feel a new energy – a spiritual upheaval that cannot be denied. 'Spirituality' is now discussed openly. Jesus, our example and way-shower, has come again to convey the wisdom of the ages, through his words at Springwell Metaphysical Studies and in books such as A Course in Miracles and New Teachings for an Awakening Humanity. Twelve master teachers have come to earth in recent years, including Archangel Gabriel who came to a small group in New York State[9] to explain the true nature of our beingness: We are all children of the Most High and now is the time to become fully aware of our God-self and express it in our daily lives. Also, many written works of spiritual guidance have been published to awaken us to this new age of enlightenment.

The 'age of reason' which humanity experienced in the eighteenth century is now supplanted by the age of spiritual awakening. For too long we have come and gone, gone and come, to and from this earth for 'experiences' in a process called reincarnation, until we have finally experienced everything our imaginations can conceive. Now is the time to seek the final frontier, the inner self, which is the kingdom of God within each of us. Science has taken us out into space, deep down into the ocean and microscopically into atomic structure. But only when we mine the gold within each of us, when we strike that holy spark we each contain, will we know peace in our lives and peace in the world – for it all begins with *you* and *me*. Thus will we discern the path back home to God.[10] This new age will bring to some a new hope, to some continuing pain, to others a challenge, to yet others a continuing and expanding joy.

Special acknowledgement is made to Archangel Gabriel for bringing to my awareness eternal truths for twelve wondrous years of learning, which resulted in the realization that I am not only a worthy human being, but also a holy child of God. And in this realization, I came to know that I was capable of writing this book. Everlasting thanks to my elder brother, Jesus the Christ for guiding me every step of the way and to the Reverend Dr. Penny A. Donovan for providing me with the essential encouragement in the production of this biography of Jesus the Christ, as well as her advanced spirituality which enabled her to bring Archangel Gabriel and the Master Jesus to us.

Specific acknowledgement is given to Mrs. Vincenza Pentick for her editorial expertise with the manuscript and infinite patience with the author throughout the editing process. Abundant thanks to Mrs. Joan Waters for her professional typing skills, proofreading expertise and editorial suggestions.

Particular acknowledgment is given to Linda Thorburn for gifting me with my first picture of The Laughing Christ; for Darryl Purinton's computer expertise that enabled early publication. Grateful appreciation is acknowledged to Susan Bray and Judy Poskanzer for reading and critiquing the manuscript.

General and grateful acknowledgment is give to Liz Williams, Kale Fiato, and Katie O'Bryan, for their interest in and reading of the manuscript. Special thanks to my dear friend Genevieve Boland, for her constant support and avid interest in this undertaking, as well as my life-long friend Mrs. Marion Polosky for her fascination with the topic and enthusiasm for reading the manuscript. Appreciation is extended to Donald Anthony, who graciously (and voluntarily) electronically prepared the manuscript for submission to the publisher.

1 Luke 15:11-32.
2 *A Course in Miracles*, Text, 622.
3 *The Aquarian Gospel of Jesus the Christ,* Introduction, 7.
4 1 Peter 2:21, I Tim. 1:16; *Aquarian Gospel*, Intro., 7.
5 *Master Jesus II.* (Rosendale, NY: Springwell, 1997) audiocassette.
6 *A Course in Miracles*, Text, 10.
7 *Aquarian Gospel*, Intro, 3.
8 Ibid, 4-5.
9 Springwell, 9/25/87-12/3/99.
10 *A Course in Miracles,* Text, 10.

INTRODUCTION

Ever since Man began walking the Earth, he has sought something outside of himself. What was he seeking? Was it an answer to 'why am I here?' or was it to substantiate his belief in his smallness, as he admired the heavens and saw countless stars that he could not touch or explain? Some of the stars seemed to form shapes of known humans or creatures and were given names five thousand years before Jesus Christ was born. We know them now as constellations, on which astrology is based.

Space ships landed and creatures disembarked and taught us how to make fire.

Of course, fire has been beneficial to the human race. Because we could not fly ourselves, we thought surely these creatures were gods, and so we listened to them and did what they suggested. We were vegetarians then. Later, other ships came with the news that it is good to eat meat. Their motive for traveling here was to find animal flesh to eat, for they had eaten all such on their own planet, to the point of beginning to eat each other. We accepted their 'news' and have partaken of animal flesh ever since.

In ancient times we received information from speakers, orators and other teachers. The power of the spoken word prevailed and any charismatic person could sway his listeners. After hieroglyphs were scrawled on cave walls, papyrus scrolls were written by a few talented scribes, for the few who could read them.

Various religions were born out of these teachers, noble and unselfish souls who cared for their fellow human beings. One of these great teachers was Jesus. Through ensuing centuries several religions were spread by word of mouth or force of arms, by zealous individuals who truly believed that killing their enemies (such as in horrendous Crusades) would promote their own dogma.

In the fifteenth century Johann Gutenberg invented the printing press, and the printed word became available to the masses. Holy creeds were put into writing and believers of each joined together in their common faith. Then a man named Martin Luther challenged the Church of Rome, by nailing 95 Theses on Indulgences to the door of a church in Wittenberg, Germany. That was the beginning of the Reformation, and dozens of protesting (Protestant) churches came into being. Today, every major religion shares some basic concepts, such as the Golden Rule. Yet the belief in separation continues, and each religion or sect believes its own to be the only, or the best one. Many religions exclude certain members of society and use their holy writings to substantiate the exclusion.

In the nineteenth century a wave of new ideas came into the faith community. These ideas were named 'New Thought' religions. Not coincidentally, they came to humanity when the ages were changing. 'New Thought' denominations were introduced as the Age of Aquarius dawned. There is a direct connection between 'New Age' and New Thought'.

In the late years of the twentieth century, twelve Master Teachers came to earth and channeled through human beings to bring the wisdom of the ages, eternal truths to humanity. These teachers have explained to us that we are not small, insignificant creatures in this vast world, covered by a vast ocean and lying beneath a vast sky, helpless to the whims of an arbitrary god or a capricious 'fate'. The truth being brought to us by these heavenly beings of Light is that we are all children of God, holy in essence, eternal in existence and perfect in manifestation. We are one with God and one with each other. Jesus brought this truth of the New Age to us, in a book entitled *A Course in Miracles*, which he describes as a 'required course.'

In addition to Archangel Gabriel, who channeled through a devout and willing minister named Rev. Penny A. Donovan, eleven other Master Teachers came to earth to bring eternal truths. In October of 1987, I was blessed to be in the company of a church congregation when Rev. Donovan began channeling an entity from the other side. Rev. Donovan was in a total trance and the voice speaking through her began with, "Beloveds of God . . . " And thus began a period of twelve years in which this voice came on a regular basis to teach us the wisdom of the ages. The singular message put to us, in a variety of stories, was that we are all children of God and must awaken to that fact, and live our lives in that knowledge. At first, the voice told us to call him Lucas. It was 1991 before the voice identified itself as Archangel Gabriel, in a seminar entitled '*Angels, Aliens and Earthlings*'. For twelve glorious years he presented daylong seminars and evening lectures. People came from Tennessee, Kentucky, New Jersey, Maine and Canada. On December 3, 1999 he bid us farewell.

The author was one of the many students who listened with profound interest to the truth put forth by Archangel Gabriel. I consider myself blessed beyond expression to have been his student. Once, at a seminar someone said to Gabriel 'I don't know who my teacher is'. Gabriel responded, 'When you find your teacher, you will know it.' This prompted me to go to the microphone and say to Archangel Gabriel, 'You are my teacher'. He looked me in the eye and said, 'And you are my student'. It was a special moment in my life. Another time he was asked if the world didn't need him longer than twelve years, considering the current strife on earth. He said that when a teacher is present, the students do not work, but when the teacher leaves, then the students go forth and spread the teachings to others. Toward the end of the twelve years, the Master Jesus also channeled through Rev. Penny, as her friends affectionately know her. Those lectures will also be referred to here and are preserved and available from Springwell Metaphysical Studies.

The purpose of this book is to tell others of the presence of Archangel Gabriel here, as well as some of his lessons. He confirmed what the Apocryphal books of the Bible told us long ago, that Jesus did not spend eighteen years working with his father as a carpenter. He traveled the known world, learning of various dogmas and teaching Our Father's truth to every race at that time. He was a man of joy. In *Jesus, Man of Joy* we find this quote: 'how could he be fully man without laughing at some of the things that happen in life? If Jesus wept, He also laughed.' (p. 27)

I will describe the man Jesus the Christ as a human being who came to earth to ground the Light of Truth to this planet; to show by his own example how to live that light and express that light which is within each of us. Nowhere in Scripture is Jesus quoted as saying, "Worship me", but there are many places in Scripture where Jesus says, "Follow me". The Kingdom of God is within each of us, for we are all created in the likeness and image of God. Note the following excerpts from Scripture, describing God as: Father of Lights (James 1:17), Spirit (John 4:24). There is a natural body and there is a spiritual body (I Cor. 15:44). Our natural body is our physical form; our spiritual body is our eternal, spiritual essence, our Higher Self. We deny the light within for it is not perceptible to human sight. No doctor, after surgery, ever said to a patient, "Behold, I saw a great light within you; it must be the kingdom of God that is spoken of in the Bible." The reason for this is given in Scripture: But the natural man receiveth not the things of the Spirit of God: for they are foolishness unto him: neither can he know them, because they are spiritually discerned. (I Cor. 2:14)

We have been taught down through the centuries that Jesus was a Man of Sorrows. I have cited passages in this book, which describe him as a man of joy and love. How could 'that holy thing' (Luke 1:35), made in the image and likeness of God and sent to be an example to us (John 13:15), with a total awareness of his Christness, have been a sorrowful man? He loved life, he loved people, and he was aware of the power of God in him – to heal, to raise the dead, to perform other miracles. But more important than the miracles was the way he lived his life from the Light within him, expressing unconditional love. He said, "Verily, verily, I say unto you, He that believeth on me, the works that I do shall he do also; and greater works than these shall he do; because I go unto my Father." (John 14:12). How could he have promised this unless it were really so?

During the crucifixion, where he is perceived as having suffered, he did not suffer. He had the ability to focus on the God-self of him and in that state he could see himself going through the motions of the torture and crucifixion. Those who have had or read about an 'out of body' experience can attest to this. He could do this only by keeping himself totally focused on his Spirit Self, which is why he did not answer when Pilate asked him, "What is truth?"

It is time on earth when we need the spiritual audacity to (1) question the old councils which rejected the apocryphal books, (2) hear the ageless wisdom from Beloved Archangel Gabriel and eleven other master teachers, (3) read the inspired and channeled writings of other teachers. We have the potential, indeed the responsibility, to seek to know our inner, spiritual selves and express them with love, forgiveness, compassion and joy. It all begins with falling in love with ourselves again – our spiritual, eternal Selves. We all came from God and His kingdom, and we shall all return to Him someday. Let us begin our wondrous, enlightened journey. I wish you Godspeed.

Chapter I: Age of Prophecy

Ever since the dawn of human consciousness, mankind has tried to pierce the curtain which separates the present from the future and to anticipate the course of coming events.

Manas, *Divination*

"Astronomers tell us that our sun and his family of planets revolve around a central sun, which is millions of miles distant, and that it requires something less than 26,000 years to make one revolution. His orbit is called the Zodiac, which is divided into twelve signs, familiarly known as Aries, Taurus, Gemini, Cancer, Leo, Virgo, Libra, Scorpio, Sagittarius, Capricorn, Aquarius and Pisces. It requires our Solar System a little more than 2,100 years to pass through one of these signs, and this time is the measurement of an Age or Dispensation. Because of what astronomers call "the precession of the Equinoxes" the movement of the sun through the signs of the Zodiac is in reverse order from that given above . . . It is conceded by all critical students that the sun entered the zodiacal sign Taurus in the days of our historic Adam when the Taurian Age began; that Abraham lived not far from the beginning of the Arian Age, when the sun entered the sign Aries. About the time of the rise of the Roman Empire the sun entered the sign Pisces, the Fishes, and the Piscean Age began, so that early in this Age Jesus of Nazareth lived."[1]

Pisces, derived from the Latin word for 'fish,' is a mutable water sign and was a symbol of the early Christians. It is personified in its own way in the Christian ritual of baptism. Following the Piscean Age came the Aquarian Age; 'Aquarius' is derived from the Latin word for water. Jesus referred to the beginning of the Aquarian Age in these words: "And then the man who bears the pitcher will walk forth across an arc of heaven; the sign and signet of the son of man will stand forth in the eastern sky. The wise will then lift up their heads and know that the redemption of the earth is near."[2]

We have moved from the Piscean Age into the Aquarian Age. In the twentieth century the hippies of the 1960's, the flower children, as they were called, awakened our world and culture – and changed them forever – to the Age of Aquarius with, among other things, an unprecedented emphasis on peace and harmony. Because Aquarius is an air sign (air being one of the four basic elements, with earth, fire and water), it is not surprising that air travel, space travel, electricity, and electronics have all been discovered and improved upon in recent decades. Most significantly, Archangel Gabriel has told us that the Aquarian Age is a spiritual age, and the people of the world are now ready to understand the deeper meaning of the profound lessons that Jesus gave to us 2,000 years ago.

'Two thousand years ago a man chose to be born to manifest in form of flesh, in awareness of mind, in the oneness of soul, the truth of the being of all life. He chose to come at a time when the ages were changing, for that was a time when vibrations around your earth can be separated, parted, rended, and caused to be broken. He came in that break and he manifested the peace that you are and the love that you are. He did this not that others might worship him but that all of you might know yourself.'[3]

Clearly, we are now coming into a more advanced stage of spiritual consciousness. Have you not noticed how frequently the word 'spirituality' has been used in the current media, literature and daily conversations? Are there not movies, television shows and books offered now about angels, their prevalence and their miracles? We are, as a human family, ready to comprehend the metaphysical side of the wonderful teachings of Jesus – teachings he intended for all humanity, not just a specific nationality or sect. All great religions share the same basic moral concepts taught by him.[4] As people of all religions come to understand and live these basic moral concepts, we will be impelled to teach them. Mary and Elizabeth were impelled to teach their sons, Jesus and John (John who became 'The Baptist' and was cousin of Jesus), as Elihu instructed them:

> Elihu said to Mary and Elizabeth, you may esteem yourselves thrice blest, for you are chosen mothers of long promised sons . . .

> We call these sons, Revealers of the Light; but they must have the light before they can reveal the light.

> And you must teach your sons, and set their souls on fire with love and holy zeal, and make them conscious of their missions to the sons of men.

> Teach them that God and man are one; but that through carnal thoughts and words and deeds, man tore himself away from God; debased himself.

> Teach that the Holy Breath would make them one again, restoring harmony and peace.

> That naught can make them one but love; that God so loved the world that he has clothed his son in flesh that man may comprehend.

> The only Savior of the world is love, and Jesus, son of Mary, comes to manifest that love to men . . .

> This age will comprehend but little of the works of Purity and Love, but not a word is lost, for in the Book of God's Remembrance a registry is made of every thought, word, and deed.

> And when the world is ready to receive, lo, God will send a messenger to open up the book and

copy from its sacred pages all the messages of Purity and Love.

Then every man of earth will read the words of life in language of his native land, and men will see the light, walk in the light, and be the light.

And man again will be at one with God.[5]

Prophecies are the foretelling of the future by those who are so attuned. In the Old Testament we find many prophecies about the coming of Jesus: Isaiah 7:14 speaks of 'Immanuel'; Isaiah 19:20 mentions 'Saviour'; Isaiah 28:16 foretells of 'a precious corner stone, a sure foundation'; Daniel 7:13 tells of the coming of the 'Son of man'; Micah 5:2 predicts a 'ruler in Israel'. In the apocryphal book of Barnabas, 111:5, we find " . . . another little one, and he shall humble three kings."

In *The Aquarian Gospel of Jesus the Christ* we find three references to these prophecies:

1. "Beyond the river Euphrates the magians lived; and they were wise, could read the language of the stars, and they divined that one, a master soul, was born; they saw his star above Jerusalem."[6]

2. "Behold, for soon the Day Star from on high will visit us, to light the way for those who sit within the darkness of the shadowland, and guide our feet unto the ways of peace."[7]

3. "And then he [Simeon] took the infant [Jesus] in his arms and said, 'Behold, this child will bring a sword upon my people, Israel, and all the world; but he will break the sword and then the nations will learn war no more. The master's cross I see upon the forehead of this child, and he will conquer by this sign'."[8]

From the chapter entitled 'The First Gospel of the Infancy of Jesus Christ', in an 1820 edition of *The Apocryphal New Testament*, we read: "The following accounts we found in

4

the book of Joseph the high priest, called by some Caiaphas:

> "He relates that Jesus spoke even when he was in his cradle, and said to his mother:
>
> 'Mary, I am Jesus the Son of God, that word which thou didst bring forth according to the declaration of the angel Gabriel to thee, and my father hath sent me for the salvation of the world'."[9]

Jesus knew from the beginning who he was and what his mission was, from birth to crucifixion and everything in between. He himself prophesied about the destruction of Jerusalem (Mark 13:1-2), his own crucifixion (Matt. 26:1-2) and his own resurrection (Mark 14:27-28). In the New Testament, Jesus speaks of his fulfilling of the prophecies: he read from Isaiah 61:1-2 in the synagogue, and then told a startled audience: "This day is this scripture fulfilled in your ears."[10]

Jesus understood prophecy; he knew that he would be the one to fulfill Isaiah's promise centuries later. Now he was confirming it. He was keenly aware that people are always seeking out others to predict the future. He also knew what we have forgotten about ourselves: that we plan our life before we come to earth and forget the plans upon our birth. Since God created us with free choice, we must ask ourselves at what point in time did he give us this free choice? If God handed us a script for our life at birth and told us that we have free choice, what sense would that make? It would seem like contradictory instructions from our Creator.

It indicates that our life is either pre-destined or we have free choice. We know that we do have free choice, therefore our free choice must begin sometime prior to our birth here on earth. But we find it far easier to ask another about our own future, as though life 'happens' to us without our participation in it.

Humankind has always sought to know the future, from sibyls and oracles in the ancient world to psychics and mediums of today. The most famous of the oracles was found at Delphi, where people of authority came from all over the known world to consult the Pythia, (the name given the woman who brought messages directly from the gods). "The Delphic Oracle enjoyed such popularity and was considered of such divine authority that people came to its shrine . . . not only from the Greek States, but from all over the ancient world."[11]

Jesus knew that the Old Testament contained many references to his coming: "And Jesus said, 'I need not tell you who I am for you have read the Law, the Prophets and the Psalms that tell of me, I am one come to break away the wall that separates the sons of men. In Holy Breath there is no Greek, nor Jew, and no Samaritan; no bond, nor free, for all are one'."[12]

In *The Aquarian Gospel of Jesus the Christ* we read that Jesus and a Grecian master named Apollo went to the Delphic Oracle, and heard the Oracle say this:

> Apollo, sage of Greece, the bell strikes twelve; the midnight of the ages now has come.
>
> Within the womb of nature ages are conceived; they gestate and are born in glory with the rising sun, and when the agic sun goes down the age disintegrates and dies.
>
> The Delphic age has been an age of glory and renown; the gods have spoken to the sons of men through oracles of wood, and gold, and precious stone.
>
> The Delphic sun has set; the Oracle will go into decline; the time is near when men will hear its voice no more.
>
> The gods will speak to man by man. The living Oracle now stands within these sacred groves; the Logos from on high has come.
>
> From henceforth will decrease my wisdom and my power; from henceforth will increase the wisdom and the power of him, Immanuel.[13]

The sibyls and oracles of Greece prophesied for a thousand years, but finally the time came when prophecy was no longer required of the human race. Indeed, the age of prophecy must come to an end, for as we tread the path which the Master Jesus tread, we shall learn of our own power, which is innate as children of the Most High. And prophecy will not be sought any longer. For then we will know that we have the power within to access the ageless wisdom of Divine Mind by attuning ourselves to God, who created us, in all wisdom, love and peace. The method to so attune ourselves is prayer and meditation. We also find the following reference to the end of the age of prophecy and prophets:

> But when in three days he comes again to the light,
>
> And shows to mortals a token, and teaches all things,
>
> Ascending in clouds will he journey to the house of Heaven,
>
> Leaving to the world the ordinance of the Gospel.
>
> Called by his name, a new shoot shall blossom forth
>
> From the Gentiles guided by the law of the Mighty.
>
> And moreover after this there shall be wise guides,
>
> And then shall be thereafter a cessation of prophets.[14]

All the while these prophetic passages were pointing to a Messiah's coming, a certain man was living out various lifetimes on earth, or incarnations, leading to the fulfillment which he came to experience: Jesus the Christ. Some of the many incarnations, which Jesus lived before achieving his Christhood, have now been revealed to us. When Jesus said, 'He that believeth on me, the works that I do shall he do also; and greater works than these shall he do; because I go unto my father,' he was saying that he came as an *example* for us, a *pattern* to follow. Search Scripture and find a place where Jesus is quoted as saying, "Worship me". You will not find it. Rather, he said, "Follow me", many times. If this be so, then is it illogical to assume the reverse situation, viz., that if we can follow in his path to attain the Christhood, then did he not first live out various incarnations

7

to his own final Christhood? And we know now that he did. Although he lived many lifetimes on earth – various earthly 'experiences' – only the incarnations in which he experienced a significant shift in his states of consciousness were described by Archangel Gabriel and will be described here.

The next chapter will review The Master's earthly lifetimes, leading up to his final earthly experience as Jesus, in which he reached his Christhood. Each of these lifetimes also represents a state of consciousness. We all move through many incarnations toward the final awakening to the Truth of what we are, until we ultimately experience that At-one-ment with God and know our own Christhood.

> The Christ is a name given to a force, to a power that is holy and divine. It has nothing to do with earth religions, nothing to do with popes or ministers or rabbis or anything of that sort. It has to do with the living Christ, which is the power within the human spirit.
>
> The Christ became grounded in the earth in the form of the man Jesus who came to the Hebrew people into a place called Jerusalem. The Hebrew people represent that aspect of humankind who holds tenaciously to the idea that there is one God. They symbolize the single-sightedness of believing in one power and one God.
>
> That belief also goes for everybody all around the world regardless of whether they are Hebrew, Gentile, or Moslem. Into the consciousness of a single God, into the idea that there is one power, we have grounded the aspect of that power which is perfect, all-encompassing love. That is what the Christ symbolizes.
>
> Springwell Metaphysical Studies'
> *I Am the Christ*, p. 5, 5/1/98

1 *Aquarian Gospel*, Intro. 3-4.
2 Ibid. 157:29-30.
3 Springwell Metaphysical Studies, *The True Meaning of Christmas*, 4-5, 12/3/95.
4 Moses, J. *Oneness.* New York: Fawcett Columbine, 1989. Also Peterson, R. *Everyone is Right.* Marina Del Rey, CA: DeVorss, 1986.
5 *Aquarian Gospel*, 7:10-28.
6 Ibid. 5:1-2.
7 Ibid. 2:26.
8 Ibid. 4:6-7.
9 Hone's *Apocryphal New Testament.* "The First Gospel of the Infancy of Jesus Christ", 1:1-3.
10 Luke 4:21.
11 *Divination Ancient and Modern,* 137.
12 *Aquarian Gospel,* 81:22-23.
13 Ibid. 45:6-11.
14 *Christian Sibyllines,* Book I. Quoted in W. Barnstone, ed. *The Other Bible,* 556.

Chapter 2: The Christs

The Christ is an active force based in love, which is very transforming. In its essence it is the love of God made manifest in humankind. It is something that, as it is used, becomes more and more until finally at last, it becomes full-blown like it did in the Master Jesus in the terms in which he used it. He was a human being who became a Christ, just as you are a human being and one day will become a Christ.

Springwell, *Master Jesus I*

As noted in chapter one, Jesus lived many, many earthly lifetimes, as every human does. Archangel Gabriel not only confirmed reincarnation as a fact rather than theory, but he explained that we all have lived so many lifetimes on earth that we have met every other human being on the planet. He told us that before we are born we decide with whom we will interact and to what degree and in what relationship, in order to learn the lessons *we* have chosen for ourselves. He said we even choose where, when, how and with who we shall die.

The key point is that this is not predestination because at any moment we have the power and choice to change our pre-birth script. In light of this information from Gabriel, we are always in charge of our lives. This means that there are no accidents and there is no such thing as 'luck', nor are we subject to the whims of an unpredictable 'fate'.

The earthly experiences of Jesus, which are described here[1] are not all of the incarnations that the Master lived;

they were the lifetimes in which he experienced a decided shift in awareness and each of these lifetimes represents a state of consciousness which all individuals must pass through on their way back home to an At-one-ment with God. "And ever since man took his place in form of flesh the Christ has been manifest in flesh at first of every age."[2]

We ourselves created 'form of flesh', for our origin and our eternal self is Spirit and Archangel Gabriel explained our origin as a time when we had no concept of evil, nor did we have need of a physical form. Our awareness was only of beauty, love, joy, and harmony – an At-one-ment with God and each other. For eons we remained in that state. That was our natural habitat; that was the way God created us. But we created our fleshly form as we decided to occupy the physical earth plane.

The Bible speaks of the beginning of Man as the presence on earth of Adam and Eve and tells the story of 'the fall' as though we fell away from God, or fell away from our own grace in God. And we now believe that God will never take us back. The Garden of Eden is an allegory. Only in our *awareness* did we 'leave God', for in fact it is impossible to leave what we are: God made manifest in flesh. Archangel Gabriel said that the most significant phrase in the story of the Garden of Eden is: "Who told you that you were naked?" and explained that it meant, "Who told you that you are less than God; separate and distinct from God and each other?"

Christian Scripture includes many stories of real people, as well as allegorical individuals. All of Scripture is subject to metaphysical interpretation. If it were not so, how could the book exist which gives the metaphysical definition of all the l names and places in Scripture? That book is *The Metaphysical Bible Dictionary,* published by Unity School of Christianity in 1931 at Unity Village, Missouri. There was no actual man named Adam. Adam represents a state of consciousness in which, as we continued to create form we came a step away from our awareness of perfection. We drifted away, in our conscious awareness, from the perfection in which we were created, and became enamored of form. We decided that solid form (flesh) was a wonderful state to be in. We forgot our way home, to the At-one-ment.

We came to believe that we no longer needed God. 'Yet the Bible (Gen. 2:21) says that a deep sleep fell upon Adam, and nowhere is there reference to his waking up. The world has not yet experienced any comprehensive reawakening or rebirth.'[3]

Jesus' incarnation as Enoch, the first of his incarnations that we will describe here, was a step on the journey of man's reawakening or rebirth. In Genesis 4:17 we find, 'And Cain knew his wife; and she conceived, and bare Enoch.' Enoch is described in *The Encyclopedia of Religion* as 'the seventh of the ten antediluvian patriarchs of Genesis, Chapter 5.' Scripture (Gen.5: 21-24) describes Enoch's lifetime:

> And Enoch lived sixty and five years, and
> begat Methuselah: And Enoch walked with
> God after he begat Methuselah three hundred
> years, and begat sons and daughters: And all
> the days of Enoch were three hundred sixty
> and five years: And Enoch walked with God:
> and he was not, for God took him.

This is a direct reference to Enoch's ascension, which is mentioned again in the New Testament: By faith Enoch was translated that he should not see death; and was not found, because God had translated him: for before his translation he had this testimony, that he pleased God.[4]

The book of Enoch is among the apocryphal books of the Bible. Enoch - which means 'He who walks with God' - still had a remembrance of the times of perfection, when all people were safe, and love and peace prevailed. However, Archangel Gabriel explained that the Enoch consciousness was greatly overshadowed by the Adam consciousness for 10,000 – 15,000 years. During this time humans were becoming aware of themselves, of other life forms and of religion, especially in Egypt, for example, where the Pharaoh named Ra first manifested the idea of one God, which was to him the Sun. Moses was the first human to manifest the idea of an abstract God.

We find the same concept in a more modern wording directed to the author of The Aquarian Gospel of Jesus the Christ:

"Now, Levi, message bearer of the Spirit Age, take up your pen and write. Write full the story of The Christ who built upon the Solid Rock of yonder circle of the sun – the Christ whom men have known as Enoch the Initiate.

Write of his works as prophet, priest and seer; write of his life of purity and love, and how he changed his carnal flesh to flesh divine without descending through the gates of death."[5]

The next incarnation of Jesus was Hermes, who came at the time of Ra, the Egyptian Sun God. Ra believed himself to be God, but it troubled him that he could not make the Sun rise or create rain. He called on Hermes to help him, for he heard that Hermes could transform anything into gold. Hermes helped Ra to learn the power of transmutation of energy, but Ra became so enthralled with himself that Hermes finally saw it was a 'lost cause'. Hermes, as an alchemist, tried to bring spirit into matter but was only partially successful because he lacked the love connectedness to do it with purity. Hermes was famous for his talent of turning anything into gold and was sought by kings to do so, but eventually he got lost in his own creative ability and was so impressed with his own popularity that he never reclaimed the Christ Love.[6]

Next, Jesus came as the personality of Melchizedek who was a Gentile, a high priest and a king. 'Melchizedek' does not appear in *The Encyclopedia of Religion* probably because he was such an ancient priest, as described in Genesis 14:18:

> . . . And Melchizedeck king of Salem
> brought forth bread and wine: and he was the
> priest of the most high God.

Only a little more information is given in Hebrews 7:1-4:

> For this Melchizedec, king of Salem, priest of
> the most high God, who met Abraham
> returning from the slaughter of the kings, and
> blessed him; To whom also Abraham gave a
> tenth part of all; first being by interpretation
> King of righteousness, and after that also King
> of Salem, which is, King of peace; Without
> father, without mother, without descent, having
> neither beginning of days nor end of life; but

made like unto the Son of God; abideth a priest
continually. Now consider how great this man
was, unto whom even the patriarch Abraham
gave the tenth of the spoils.

Melchizedek knew that we teach what we need to learn, and
this time he was determined to overcome his ego. He knew
the consciousness of Abraham but could not reach it.
Abraham had *faith* in the unseen. Melchizedek had
knowledge of the unseen. Melchizedek knew that all that is
seen comes from what is unseen. He lifted up the
consciousness of man, by bringing external to internal. It
was this consciousness that introduced the ritual of Holy
Communion to humankind. Ritual was extremely important
then (several centuries before Christ). People's minds were
dull; they believed in sacrifice, as did Abraham, who was
ready to sacrifice his own son (Genesis 14:18). So that
people could become aware, by way of a ritual, that the
connectedness to God comes not from external sacrifice but
from the internal self, Holy Communion was introduced.
Bread was the staff of life to nomads; they could travel with it
without its spoiling quickly. It could be made anywhere.
Thus, bread could be symbolic of the substance of life from
which everything comes forth. Wine represented blood, or
the continuing flow of life. So the Substance of God of All,
plus eternalness, were what people of that time could
comprehend. Melchizedek introduced the idea of Holy
Communion to Abraham and Abraham introduced the idea
to the people. The bread and wine represented the *internal*
connectedness to God (already within, but people then
believed that they had to *do* something). It was believed
then that you ate what you desired to be, i.e. if you wanted to
be powerful, you ate lion meat; if you wanted to be strong,
you ate bull; to increase faith in God, you ate lamb. Thus,
the bread had to be specifically made for the ritualistic
purpose of Communion, and the wine had to be the finest.
Jesus, as Melchizedek, saw this ritual as a way to 'get it into
their heads' about the internalness of spiritual life.[7] Other
scriptural phrases describe Melchizedek: And Melchizedek
king of Salem brought forth bread and wine: and he was the
priest of the most high God.[8] Also: The Lord hath sworn, and

will not repent, Thou art a priest for ever after the order of Melchizedek.[9]

Not only is Melchizedek mentioned in Psalms, but the prophecy is reiterated two thousand years later in *The Aquarian Gospel*, 128:27: "And John spoke out and said, 'When we were in Jerusalem I heard a seer exclaim, This Jesus is none other than Melchizedek, the king of peace, who lived about two thousand years ago, and said that he would come again'." In very eloquent poetry, we find this prophecy in *The Voice Celestial:*

> Behind the altar in rainbowed arcs of light,
> I saw a priest, arrayed in silver-white,
> Melchizedek, eternal priest and king
> Of righteousness and peace, outrivaling
> All priests of all the altars of the earth,
> Who could not die nor had he second birth
> But wore the miter placed upon his brow
> By LIFE and not by LAW and took the vow
> Of fealty to God from all the saints and sages
> As he had done throughout the endless ages;
> Not Jesus only but every seer to wait
> Before the shrine had been initiate
> of the Order of Melchizedek.[10]

The next incarnation of the Master was Joseph, son of Jacob and Rachel, (Gen. 35:22-24) whose brothers sold him into slavery. (Gen. 37:28) As we read the full story of Joseph we find that he forgave his brothers years later for their betrayal (Gen. 45:1-5). Archangel Gabriel explained that this forgiving act was the very first expression on earth of the forgiveness consciousness that used love rather than vengeance. Joseph represents light entering darkness. Joseph restored life to his brothers, never reminding them of the way they had treated him. Joseph, in effect, said, "You intended evil, but God intended Good – for only Good is God's intent from the beginning." [11]

Joshua was Jesus' next incarnation. Joshua, son of Nun, was Moses' minister. When Moses was in the desert he knew what he wanted to do but not how to put it into action. He ardently desired to please God, but feared his actions would offend God. He asked Joshua for help and said to him, "Get these people to the Promised Land."

Joshua had a warrior mentality and he had vast power, including the ability to read the signs of the earth. Moses had great power, but hesitated to take action. Joshua relished a battle and was happy to comply with Moses' request to reach the Promised Land with Moses' followers. Joshua recalled Moses' separating the Red Sea and so he tuned into the earth's vibration and discerned that an earthquake was coming. When he arrived at the river, he heard an angel suggest that he use the Ark of the Covenant. So Joshua sent the Ark out into the water with the carriers, wondering if they would drown. About ten miles upriver, the earthquake hit and stopped the flow of water so that Moses and his people could cross. Jerusalem's warriors had chariots with spoked wheels that could chop their enemies to pieces; Joshua was fully aware of this fact, but he also knew that chariots could not be taken into the hills, where there were many towns. Joshua, with an abundance of manpower behind him, took the battle to his chosen territory and sacked the towns in the mountains, plundering everything. He told the men 'Take no prisoners' and all the townspeople - men, women and children - were killed. Joseph was the forgiver, Joshua the slaughterer. The total slaughter represents the elimination of all thoughts of limitation. Joshua rid the human consciousness of limitation and brought it to the Promised Land - Christ consciousness.[12] Christ consciousness is spirit manifested; it has nothing to do with Christianity; Christ consciousness is for all people. "(Every knee shall bow . . ." in Rom.14: 11, means every illusion will bow to the Almighty God). We must get rid of all our misperceptions.[13]

The penultimate incarnation of Jesus was Buddha. As a royal prince Buddha was born to wealth and lived a protected life within the temple walls. After he married and had a child, one day he decided to travel outside the temple and for the first time saw death, disease, poverty and hunger. He could not understand how these things could be and embarked on a quest to learn. He felt that there was more to life than what the physical offered and that in that lay the meaning of life. He knew in his mind what he could not take into his heart. He so totally desired to know God that he allowed nothing to divert his attention from his goal. He left his wife and child, rejected all comforts, wore ragged clothes and stopped eating until he nearly destroyed his intestines. He went to a pool and beheld his image and thought, 'I am thin and wretched and I still do not understand'. So he dressed, ate and concluded that the outside world was not giving him an answer. He decided to 'go within' and he began to meditate. Others saw him sitting silently by the hour and thought him a guru. They brought him food and listened to him. He learned one great truth: that compassion, respect, love for ALL LIFE was the only way to leave behind one's karma – not to build any karma by negative thinking. At that time, in the 6th century BC, there were two teachings: the Vedas (the law) and the Upanishads, which addressed the internalness of God. Buddha did not always sit under a tree, as he is often depicted. He walked and helped others. Once he found a beggar, filthy and uncared for. He carried him to the river, washed and clothed him, and said, "Be kind always, because what you do to others comes to you." Kindness is an attribute of the Christ consciousness of God. Buddha taught the soul how to live these truths – truths and teachings that are almost identical with Jesus' teachings. There were those who recognized the similarity. We find in *The Aquarian Gospel of Jesus the Christ*, the priests in Kapivastu, India said, "Is this not Buddha come again in flesh? No other one could speak with such simplicity and power."[14]

After Jesus' incarnation as Buddha, he had a total understanding of human needs – compassion and forgiveness. On the astral plane after the Buddha incarnation, he contemplated how he had brought these aspects of himself into understanding and how he could bring them to fullness. He understood the lessons he had learned. Then, Gabriel informs us, he spent five hundred years of earth time, surrendering absolutely to the Will of God.[15]

Then he incarnated as Jesus. Archangel Gabriel, in *Master Jesus I*, summarizes these incarnations of Jesus. He knew he had to come back one more time in flesh, walk among humanity and express what he *was* and not what he *knew*. As Hermes, he knew how to manipulate energy. As Melchizedek, he took the spiritual to the ritual which people would understand. As Joseph, he learned love and forgiveness. As Joshua, he went to the hidden places (Jericho) of consciousness and annihilated all error perception (fear). As Buddha, he learned how to discern what *appears* to be and what one needed to know that was *real*: the At-one-ment. Now he had to pull it all together whereby learning and experiences could be manifested on all levels as courage and wisdom – he had to bring all that he had learned into the fold of human consciousness and establish forever the Christ consciousness on earth. Scripture tells us the lost sheep parable (Luke 15:3-7) in which one sheep was lost and ninety-nine were all right. The shepherd rejoiced at finding the one lost sheep more than having the ninety-nine. Jesus, our shepherd, went to the hills of death and disillusionment to bring each one of us, as well as himself, into the fold of awareness.[16]

Archangel Gabriel explained to us that Buddha considered wisdom the paramount goal in life, but from his perspective on the other side after resurrecting, he realized that the paramount goal in life is love, and so he came as Jesus to demonstrate it.

> Then Jesus came, the last to take his place
> In that great line of masters of the race
> To shed his radiance upon the saints and sages
> Who bowed before the Altar of the Ages[17]

The words of Archangel Gabriel were sometimes difficult to accept, such as when he told us that 'all pain is self-inflicted', since we plan every person and circumstance in our lives and have free choice to change them at will. Most of the time his words were very comforting, as in the following: "The power of Christ is on your earth now. What was grounded 2,000 years ago is now producing a harvest – the ability to become what he was years ago and see the results of what occurred at that time. You have this to come to: the Jesus State of Consciousness."[18] Turning now to Emmanuel's Book, we find this idea in poetic verse:

The greater reality

which you have all touched in meditation and prayer,

truly coexists in the same space

where your cars and your boats,

your water and your parks

and your rain and yourselves also sit.

In that expanded reality

that shares all eternity with you

Christ is alive and well

and walks among you.[19]

This Christ, this love of God, transforms everything. But the first step we must take is acknowledge its truth, and then put some spiritual muscle into seeking and finding that truth in our own lives. Only then can we live with our lights shining forth, guiding others to that magnificent truth.

"You are *already* a God. *You simply do not know it.* Have I not said, 'Ye are Gods'?"[20]

1 *Master Jesus I.* (Rosendale, NY: Springwell, 1997), audiocassette.
2 *Aquarian Gospel*, Intro. 7.
3 *A Course in Miracles,* Text, 15.
4 Hebrews 11:5.
5 *Aquarian Gospel*, Intro, 9.
6 *Master Jesus I.*
7 *Master Jesus I.*
8 Gen. 14:18.
9 Psalm 110:4.
10 *The Voice Celestial*, 199.
11 *Master Jesus I.*
12 Ibid.
13 Ibid.
14 *Aquarian Gospel* 34:4.
15 *Master Jesus I.*
16 Ibid.
17 *The Voice Celestial,* 270.
18 *Master Jesus I.*
19 *Emmanuel's Book,* 238.
20 *Conversations with God,* Book I, 202; Psalm 82:6; John 10:34.

Chapter 3: Birth and Childhood

Christ was the joyous boy of the fields. We are not permitted to think that the shadows of Calvary darkened His pathway as a youth, and the Apocryphal Books of the New Testament show a great deal of the early life of Christ not to be found in the four Evangelists.

Dr. Talmadge, *The Lost Books of the Bible*

The term 'immaculate conception' is a concept difficult to believe based on our understanding of the natural human process of conception. But let us look at some of the writings about this more specifically. Mary entered a cloistered life at the age of three and lived a very sheltered existence. Mary prepared herself mentally by thinking of an 'Ideal Person'. She had the ability to love enough to bring forth something holy. She adhered to a physical diet and a way of life to prepare the cells of her body with an energy unit so loved and known that she was accepting of the spirit overshadowing her to manifest perfection in her. Jesus worked with Mary from the spirit realm and their combined energy created the Son of God.[1]

As we look at "The Infancy Gospel of James" we find Joseph on his journey with Mary and an experience just prior to Jesus' birth:

> He saddled his donkey and set Mary upon it;
> his son led, and Samuel followed. They drew
> near to Bethlehem – they were three miles
> distant – and Joseph turned and saw Mary

looking gloomy, and he said, "Probably that which is in her is distressing her." Once again Joseph turned and saw her laughing, and he said, "Mary, how is it that I see your face at one moment laughing and at another time gloomy?" She said to Joseph "It is because I see two peoples with my eyes, the one weeping and mourning, the other rejoicing and glad." . . . He found there a cave, and he brought her in and placed his sons beside her. Then he went out to seek a Hebrew midwife in the country of Bethlehem. [2]

Following this glimpse into the relationship between Mary and Joseph, we hear Joseph reveal to us his mystical experience as he sought a midwife:

Now I, Joseph, was walking about, and I looked up and saw the Heaven standing still, and I observed the air in amazement, and the birds of Heaven at rest. Then I looked down at the earth, and I saw a vessel lying there, and workmen reclining, and their hands were in the vessel. Those who were chewing did not chew, and those who were lifting did not lift up, and those who were carrying to their mouths did not carry, but all faces were looking upward. I saw sheep standing still, and the shepherd raised his hand to strike them, and his hand remained up. I observed the streaming river; and I saw the mouths of the kids at the water, but they were not drinking. Then suddenly all things were driven in their course.[3]

There are various stories about the moment of birth of Jesus. It is difficult to choose which ones to present, and it is difficult to present them in chronological order. However, because they are all so poignant, I present them here.

Having found a midwife, Joseph said to her,

Mary is the one who was betrothed to me, but she, having been brought up in the Temple of the Lord, has conceived by the Holy Spirit . . ..

They stood in the place of the cave, and a dark cloud was overshadowing the cave. The midwife said, "My soul is magnified today, for my eyes have seen a mystery: a Savior has been born to Israel!" And immediately the cloud withdrew from the cave, and a great light appeared in the cave so that their eyes could not bear it. After a while the light withdrew, until the baby appeared. It came and took the breast of its mother Mary; and the midwife cried out, "How great is this day, for I have seen this new wonder!"

The midwife went in and placed Mary in position and [Salome entered the cave and] examined her virginal nature; and Salome cried aloud that she had tempted the living God – "and behold, my hand falls away from me in fire." Then she prayed to the Lord.

Behold, an angel of the Lord appeared, saying to Salome, "Your prayer has been heard before the Lord God. Come near and take up the child, and this will save you." She did so; and Salome was healed as she worshipped. Then she came out of the cave. Behold an angel of the Lord spoke, saying, "Salome, Salome, do not report what marvels you have seen until the child has come into Jerusalem."[4]

Another look at the moment of the birth of Jesus is related in "A Latin Infancy Gospel":

"For hours Mary permitted herself to be watched, then the midwife cried with a loud voice and said, 'Lord, great God, have mercy, because never has this been heard, nor seen, nor even dreamed of, until now, that the breasts should be full of milk and a male child, after birth, should make his mother known to be a virgin. There was no offering of blood in the birth, no pain occurred in the parturition. A virgin conceived, a virgin has given birth and after she gave birth she remained a virgin'."

The midwife was then asked to relate to Symeon, Joseph's son, what she had seen.

> When I entered to the maiden, I found her face looking upward; she was inclined toward Heaven and speaking to herself. I truly believe that she prayed to and blessed the Most High. When I had come to her, I said "Daughter, tell me, do you not feel some pain, or is not some part of your body gripped with pain?" She, however, as if she heard nothing, remained immobile like solid rock, intent on Heaven.

> In that hour, everything ceased. There was total silence and fear. For even the winds stopped, they made no breeze; there was no motion of tree leaves; no sound of water was heard. The streams did not flow; there was no motion of the sea. All things produced in the water were quiet; there was no human voice sounding; there was a great silence. For the pole itself ceased its rapid course from that hour. Time almost stopped its measure. All, overwhelmed with great fear, kept silent; we were expecting the advent of the most high God, the end of the world.

> As the time drew near, the power of God showed itself openly . . . When the light had come forth, Mary worshipped him to whom she saw she had given birth. The child himself, like the sun, shone bright, beautiful, and was most delightful to see, because he alone appeared as peace, soothing the whole world. In that hour, when he was born, the voice of many invisible beings in one voice proclaimed "Amen." And the light, when it was born, multiplied, and it obscured the light of the sun itself by its shining rays. The cave was filled by the bright light together with a most sweet odor. The light was born just as the dew

descends from Heaven to the earth. For its odor is fragrant beyond all the sweet smell of ointments.

I, however, stood stupefied and amazed. Awe grasped me. I was gazing intently at the fantastically bright light which had been born. The light, however, after a while, shrank, imitated the shape of an infant, then immediately became outwardly an infant in the usual manner of born infants. I became bold and leaned over and touched him. I lifted him in my hands with great awe, and I was terrified because he had no weight like other babies who are born. I looked at him closely; there was no blemish on him, but he was in his body totally shining, just as the dew of the most high God. He was light to carry, splendid to see. For a while I was amazed at him because he did not cry as newborn children are supposed to. While I held him, looking into his face, he laughed at me with a most joyful laugh, and, opening his eyes, he looked intently at me. Suddenly a great light came forth from his eyes like a great flash of lightning.[5]

These are such glorious visions of the observers at the moment of the birth, and clearly indicate the divinity of the child Jesus. The shepherds, too, had a magnificent experience when they arrived at the cave: "After this, when the shepherds came, and had made a fire, and they were exceedingly rejoicing, the heavenly host appeared to them, praising and adoring the supreme God . . .

The cave at that time seemed like a glorious temple, because both the tongues of angels and men united to adore and magnify God, on account of the birth of the Lord Christ."[6]

In the Apocrypha we find a most interesting story of the three wise men that came to see the infant Jesus, and their experience upon returning home:

And it came to pass, when the Lord Jesus was born at Bethlehem, a city of Judea, in the time of Herod the King; the wise men came from the East to Jerusalem, according to the prophecy of Zorodascht (Zoroaster), and brought with them offerings: namely, gold, frankincense, and myrrh, and worshipped him, and offered to him their gifts.

Then the Lady Mary took one of his swaddling clothes in which the infant was wrapped, and gave it to them instead of a blessing, which they received from her as a most noble present . . .

On their return their kings and princes came to them inquiring, What had they seen and done? What sort of journey and return they had? What company they had on the road?

But they produced the swaddling cloth which St. Mary had given to them, on account whereof they kept a feast.

And having, according to the custom of their country, made a fire, they worshipped it.

And casting the swaddling cloth into it, the fire took it, and kept it.

And when the fire was put out, they took forth the swaddling cloth unhurt, as much as if the fire had not touched it.[7]

The metaphysical significance of the virgin birth of Jesus is expressed succinctly in *Emmanuel's Book* as follows:

Christ's birth
is the kiss of eternal love.
It is one of the greatest gifts
that God has given to humanity.
It is the symbol in human form
of the eternal reality of God,
His love, His nurturing,
and what has been termed His intervention.[8]

The powers of Jesus in his infancy, and his ability to care for his parents before he could even walk, are described with exquisite clarity in an apocryphal text:

> The infant Jesus, still at his mother's breast in the third day of his life, hears that his mother is hungry and thirsty. He orders a palm tree to bend down, which it does, so his mother can gather fruit from it. Then he orders it to raise itself to be a companion of trees in Heaven, whereupon fountains of water pour out from its roots to refresh his family.

> The child also . . . shortens the thirty-day trip across the desert to Egypt into a single day. In Egypt when Mary and Jesus enter a religious temple, the three hundred and sixty-five idols immediately fall to the ground and shatter. The governor is so impressed that he and the entire city of Egyptians convert to the true Lord God.[9]

These miraculous accomplishments of Jesus are no more difficult for us to believe than the miracles of healing leprosy and blindness, or raising the dead that Jesus did years later. The wonderment now is that the stories were not considered important enough to be included in the accepted canon for future generations. There are many stories about Jesus' infancy. Only a few of them are given here.

> Then after ten days they brought him to Jerusalem, and on the fortieth day from his birth they presented him in the temple before the Lord, making the proper offerings for him, according to the requirement of the law of Moses: namely, that every male which opens the womb shall be called holy unto God.

> At that time old Simeon saw him shining as a pillar of light, when St. Mary the Virgin, his mother, carried him in her arms, and was filled with the greatest pleasure at the sight.

> And the angels stood around him, adoring him, as a king's guards stand around him.

Then Simeon going near to St. Mary, and stretching forth his hands towards her, said to the Lord Christ, Now, O my lord, thy servant shall depart in peace, according to thy word;

For mine eyes have seen thy mercy, which thou hast prepared for the salvation of all nations; a light to all people, and the glory of thy people Israel.

Hannah the prophetess was also present, and drawing near, she gave praises to God, and celebrated the happiness of Mary.[10]

From another source, we find Simeon and an aged widow tell of their joy at seeing the infant Jesus and their recognition of the sign of the cross on his forehead:

A pious Jew named Simeon was in the temple serving God.

From early youth he had been looking for Immanuel to come, and he had prayed to God that he might not depart until his eyes had seen Messiah in the flesh.

And when he saw the infant Jesus he rejoiced and said, I now am ready to depart in peace, for I have seen the king . . .

The master's cross I see upon the forehead of this child, and he will conquer by this sign.

And in the temple was a widow, four and eighty years of age, and she departed not, but night and day she worshipped God.

And when she saw the infant Jesus she exclaimed, Behold Immanuel! Behold the signet cross of the Messiah on his brow!

And then the woman knelt to worship him, as God with us, Immanuel; but one, a master, clothed in white, appeared and said,

Good woman, stay; take heed to what you do; you may not worship man; this is idolatry.

This child is man, the son of man, and worthy
of all praise. You shall adore and worship
God; him only shall you serve.[11]

Jesus' power of healing, even as a child, was extended in
many ways to several people, as Mary and Joseph
journeyed with him through Egypt. These events are
described in detail in *The Apocryphal New Testament,* The
First Gospel of the Infancy of Jesus Christ, Books I and II.
Only one such event is described here:

In their journey . . . They came into a desert
country, and were told it was infested with
robbers; so Joseph and St. Mary prepared to
pass through it in the night.

And as they were going along, behold they
saw two robbers asleep in the road, and with
them a great number of robbers, who were
their confederates, also asleep.

The names of these two were Titus and
Dumachus; and Titus said to Dumachus, I
beseech thee, let those persons go along
quietly, that our company may not perceive
anything of them:

But Dumachus refusing, Titus again said, I will
give thee forty groats, and as a pledge take my
girdle, which he gave him before he had done
speaking, that he might not open his mouth, or
make a noise.

When the Lady St. Mary saw the kindness
which this robber did shew them, she said to
him, The Lord God will receive thee to his right
hand, and grant thee pardon of thy sins.

Then the Lord Jesus answered, and said to
his mother, When thirty years are expired, O
mother, the Jews will crucify me at Jerusalem;

And these two thieves shall be with me at the
same time upon the cross, Titus on my right
hand, and Dumachus on my left, and from that

time Titus shall go before me into paradise . . [12]

Prophecies that Jesus made as a child indicate that not only did he know what his future would be but who would participate in it with him. He was obviously aware that he could impart this knowledge to his mother, knowing that she would understand.

Archangel Gabriel told us a wonderful story about the boy Jesus on December 3, 1999, in *Gabriel's Farewell Message,* p.25 (Springwell Metaphysical Studies):

> Know what the Master did one time when he was about four years old? He had been to the temple listening to the elders and they were talking about the spirit of God. Since he always had this sense of the presence of God, he went out, sat down, and thought about it. He thought about God as life, as the beingness. And even though he was but a little fellow, he thought if God is life and God is eternal, then life is eternal. So the death of a form, of a body has nothing to do with the livingness of life.

> Jesus figured this all out in his little boy brain. So he decided to try it out. If life always is, then life can be called back into form. As he was sitting there very still doing all of this thinking, some little birds came and gathered around his feet. So he picked up a stone and whacked one over the head and killed it. Then he put his little hands upon it and said, "I restore you to life through the power of God in me." And the little bird got up and flew away . . . he restored the bird to life.

> So the Master Jesus went home and said to his mother, "I just brought a bird back to life."

> His mother, being as wise as she was, turned around and said, "And how did it get dead?" He told her. She said, "You can't go around beating little birds over the head."

30

"Oh, but you don't understand. I brought it back to life."

She said, "All right, you know you can do that. Now don't do that again."

Chapter XIV of The First Gospel of the Infancy of Jesus Christ tells us of a boy who was possessed and who bit those around him and if no one was about, he bit himself. One day he was about to bite Jesus.

"And because he could not do it, he struck Jesus on the right side, so that Jesus cried out, and the boy ran away . . .

"This same boy who struck Jesus was Judas Iscariot, who betrayed him to the Jews.

"And that same side, on which Judas struck him, the Jews pierced with a spear."[13]

It is amazing to this author that there are so many anecdotal stories about Jesus as a child which make fascinating reading and illustrate the various traits and abilities which he possessed.

> When this child Jesus was five years old, he was playing at the ford of a stream. He made pools of the rushing water and made it immediately pure; he ordered this by word alone. He made soft clay and modeled twelve sparrows from it. It was the Sabbath when he did this. There were many other children playing with him. A certain Jew saw what Jesus did while playing on the Sabbath; he immediately went and announced to his father Joseph, "See, your child is at the stream, and has taken clay and modeled twelve birds; he has profaned the Sabbath." Joseph came to the place, and seeing what Jesus did he cried out, "Why do you do on the Sabbath what it is not lawful to do?" Jesus clapped his hands and cried to the sparrows, "Be gone." And the sparrows flew off chirping.[14]

Jesus performed many miracles as a child, 'practicing' for the miracles he would perform as a magnificent teacher and healer when he matured. But he also was knowledgeable about the etymology of his native language to the point of giving a treatise to his teacher, Zaccheus, about the letters of the alphabet, their structure and form:

> A man named Zaccheus, a teacher, . . . approached Joseph and said to him, "You have a smart child, and he has a mind. Come, hand him over to me so that he may learn writing. I will give him all understanding with the letters, and teach him to greet all the elders and to honor them as grandfathers and fathers and to love his peers." He told him all the letters from the Alpha to the Omega plainly, with much discussion. But Jesus looked at Zaccheus the teacher, and said to him, "You do not know the Alpha according to nature, how do you teach others the Beta? You hypocrite! First, if you know it, teach the Alpha, then we shall believe you about the Beta." Then he began to question the teacher about the first letter and he could not answer him. Many heard as the child said to Zaccheus, "Listen, teacher, to the order of the first element, and pay attention to this, how it has lines, and a central mark which goes through the two lines you see, they converge, go up, again come to head, become the same three times, subordinate, and hypostatic, isometric . . . You now have the lines of Alpha."[15]

At this, Zaccheus laments his situation at length. In part, he said, "I cannot bear the severity of his glance. I cannot understand his speech at all. This child is not earth-born; he is able to tame even fire. Perhaps he was begotten before the world's creation. What belly bore him, what womb nurtured him, I do not know.

"Woe is me, friend, he completely confuses me . . . I worked anxiously to have a disciple, and I found myself with a teacher. I consider my shame, friends; I am an old man and have been conquered by a child, . . . what can I say?. . . he is something great: a God, an angel, or what I should say I do not know."[16]

Another example of Jesus' miracles, one in which he raises a child in the neighborhood from the dead, follows: "After some days Jesus was playing upstairs in a certain house, and one of the children playing with him fell from the house and died. And when the other children saw this they ran away, and Jesus remained alone. The parents of the dead child came and accused Jesus of throwing him down. Jesus replied, 'I did not throw him down.' But still they accused him. Then Jesus leaped down from the roof and stood by the body of the child and cried out in a great voice, saying 'Zenon . . . Rise up and tell me, did I throw you down?' He immediately rose up and said: 'No, Lord, you did not throw me down, but you raised me'."[17] This story clearly indicates that his peers, though they were playmates with Jesus, accepted him as their Lord. Both of Jesus' parents were often astonished at the boy's ability to do miraculous things on a daily basis, with ordinary situations.

> When (Jesus) was six, his mother sent him to draw water and to bring it into the house, giving him a pitcher. But in the crowd, he had a collision; the water jug was broken. Jesus spread out the garment he had on, filled it with water, and bore it to his mother. When his mother saw the miracle she kissed him, and she kept to herself the mysteries which she saw him do . . . His father was a carpenter and at that time made ploughs and yokes. He received an order from a certain rich man to make a bed for him. One beam came out shorter than the other, and he did not know what to do. The child Jesus said to Joseph his father, "Lay the two pieces of wood alongside each other, and make them even at one end." Joseph did as the child told him. Jesus stood at the other end and grasped the shorter beam; he stretched it and made it equal with the other. His father Joseph saw and was astonished, and embracing the child he kissed

him and said, "I am blessed because God has given this child to me."[18]

There are other stories about Jesus' ability to bail out his father when Joseph made a mistake in measuring wood. This might indicate that Joseph was only a mediocre carpenter, but Gabriel has made it abundantly clear that Joseph was a very good father to Jesus and Jesus loved him dearly. As a boy and as a man, Jesus always loved and respected his parents, and whenever he was in their presence he respectfully honored them. Jesus also loved his older brothers, and one time had the opportunity to save one from death.

"Joseph sent his older son James to gather wood . . . Jesus followed him. While James was gathering the sticks, a snake bit his hand. As he lay dying, Jesus came near and breathed on the bite. Immediately James ceased suffering, the snake burst, and James was healed."

Another time a neighbor's son took sick and died. "His mother wept bitterly. Jesus, hearing the great mourning and clamor, ran quickly and found the child dead. He touched his breast and said, 'I say to you, child, do not die, but live and be with your mother!' And immediately the child looked up and laughed. Jesus said to the woman, 'Pick him up and give him milk, and remember me'."[19]

It is interesting to note that there were times when Jesus as a child said 'remember me' and as an adult he often said, 'tell no one of this' after he performed a miracle. Apparently he wanted his boyhood friends and neighbors to know him so that when he matured and taught he would be known as a teacher of eternal truths rather than a performer of miracles. Miracles excite us momentarily, but learning to live from the Lord God of our Being takes practice and dedication.

All Jesus' behaviors as a child, whether as a divine prankster or a divine healer, were in preparation for his ministry, when he would teach the disciples. The power that he possessed, he desired to pass on to the disciples. One of the ways he revealed his power as a child was illustrated when he went into the dyer's shop, took all the cloths and threw them in the furnace. When Salem, the dyer, came home, he saw the cloths spoiled and began to rave at Jesus, saying, 'What hast thou done to me? . . . Thou hast injured both me and my neighbors; they all desired their cloths of a proper color; but thou hast come and spoiled them all.' Jesus replied, 'I will change the color of every cloth to what color thou desirest.' . . . He took the cloths out of the furnace, and they were all dyed of the same colors which the dyer desired.[20] Because of Jesus' mischievous ways, he often got into trouble and sometimes the people feared him for his power. It was Joseph's task to show the young Jesus how to use his power carefully and with discretion. Jesus was teachable and so he learned. Jesus loved Joseph dearly and often went with him to do carpentry work or just to be 'doing what men do'.[21]

Because of this closeness to his father and his great love for his parents and extended family, it must have been difficult indeed for him to leave his home and dear ones to travel on long journeys. This is another example of the depth of his love and concern for humanity – that it precluded his personal attachment to relatives. It calls to mind the Scripture which reads "He that loveth father or mother more than me is not worthy of me . . ." (Matthew 10:37). The 'me' to which he referred is the Christ Love, and once again he demonstrated by his own actions – giving up the presence of family in order to reach into the Christ Self -that everyone can do the same.

When Jesus' seventh birthday arrived, Joachim, his grandfather, told Jesus he could have any gift he chose. Jesus said that the finest gift he could receive would be to invite all the needy children of Nazareth to a banquet. He was given permission, and he hurried all through the town to announce it. "And in a little time one hundred and three score of happy ragged boys and girls were following him up Marmion Way."[22]

As a child, Jesus was willing to share his visionary dreams with his beloved parents and grandparents. And he did so with an expressive vocabulary.

The home of Joseph was on Marmion Way in
Nazareth; here Mary taught her son the
lessons of Elihu and Salome.

And Jesus greatly loved the Vedic hymns and
the Avesta; but more than all he loved to read
the Psalms of David and the pungent words of
Solomon.

The Jewish books of prophecy were his
delight; and when he reached his seventh year
he needed not the books to read, for he had
fixed in memory every word.

Joachim and his wife, grandparents of child
Jesus, made a feast in honor of the child, and
all their near of kin were guests.

And Jesus stood before the guests and said, I
had a dream, and in my dream I stood before a
sea, upon a sandy beach.

The waves upon the sea were high; a storm
was raging on the deep.

Someone above gave me a wand. I took the
wand and touched the sand, and every grain of
sand became a living thing; the beach was all a
mass of beauty and of song.

I touched the waters at my feet, and they were
changed to trees, and flowers, and singing
birds, and every thing was praising God.

And someone spoke, I did not see the one who
spoke, I heard the voice, which said, There is
no death.

Anna, Jesus' grandmother, loved her dear grandson. She
put her hand on Jesus' head and interpreted his dream for
him:

I saw you stand beside the sea; I saw you
touch the sand and waves; I saw them turn to
living things and then I knew the meaning of
the dream.

The sea of life rolls high; the storms are great.
The multitude of men are idle, listless, waiting,
like dead sand upon the beach.

Your wand is truth. With this you touch the
multitudes, and every man becomes a
messenger of holy light and life.

You touch the waves upon the sea of life; their
turmoils cease; the very winds become a song
of praise.

There is no death, because the wand of truth
can change the dryest bones to living things,
and bring the loveliest flowers from stagnant
ponds, and turn the most discordant notes to
harmony and praise.[23]

This passage indicates that Jesus at an early age was aware
of his great mission on earth. The fact that his grandmother
interpreted the dream indicates her part in the realization of
his purpose as well as explaining to Jesus the magnitude of
his mission and the universal impact it would have. Jesus
had no problem confronting his elders, whether they were
priests or teachers. Whenever he saw an injustice, he spoke
up boldly against it. When Jesus was ten he went to
Jerusalem with his kin for the great feast.

And Jesus watched the butchers kill the lambs
and birds and burn them on the altar in the
name of God.

His tender heart was shocked at this display of
cruelty; he asked the serving priests, What is
the purpose of this slaughter of the beasts and
birds? Why do you burn their flesh before the
Lord?

The priests replied, This is our sacrifice for sin.
God has commanded us to do these things,
and said that in these sacrifices all our sins are
blotted out.

And Jesus said, Will you be kind enough to tell
me when God proclaimed that sins are blotted
out by sacrifice of any kind?

Did not David say that God requires not a sacrifice for sin; that it is sin itself to bring before his face burnt offerings, as offerings for sin? Did not Isaiah say the same?

The priest replied, My child, you are beside yourself. Do you know more about the laws of God than all the priests of Israel? This is no place for boys to show their wit.

But Jesus heeded not his taunts; he went to Hillel, chief of the Sanhedrin, and he said to him,

Rabboni, I would like to talk with you; I am disturbed about this service of the pascal feast. I thought the temple was the house of God where love and kindness dwell.

Do you not hear the bleating of those lambs, the pleading of those doves that men are killing over there? Do you not smell that awful stench that comes from burning flesh?

Can man be kind and just, and still be filled with cruelty?

A God that takes delight in sacrifice, in blood and burning flesh, is not my Father-God.

I want to find a God of love, and you, my master, you are wise, and surely you can tell me where to find the God of love.

But Hillel could not give an answer to the child. His heart was stirred with sympathy. He called the child to him; he laid his hand upon his head and wept.

He said, There is a God of love, and you shall come with me; and hand in hand we will go forth and find the God of love.

And Jesus said, Why need we go? I thought that God is everywhere. Can we not purify our hearts and drive out cruelty, and every wicked thought, and make within, a temple where the God of love can dwell?

The master of the great Sanhedrin felt as though he was himself the child, and that before him stood Rabboni, master of the higher law.

 He said within himself, This child is surely prophet sent from God.

Then Hillel sought the parents of the child, and asked that Jesus might abide with him, and learn the precepts of the law, and all the lessons of the temple priests.

 His parents gave consent, and Jesus did abide within the holy temple in Jerusalem, and Hillel taught him every day. And every day the master learned from Jesus many lessons of the higher life.

The child remained with Hillel in the temple for a year, and then returned unto his home in Nazareth; and there he wrought with Joseph as a carpenter.[24]

The story of Jesus remaining behind in the temple when he was twelve is told in Scripture (Luke 2:42-49). The following gives more detail as to the conversation between Jesus and the rabbis: "And he explained to them the books of the law, and precepts, and statutes: and the mysteries which are contained in the books of the prophets; things which the mind of no creature could reach.

"Then said that Rabbi, 'I never yet have seen or heard of such knowledge! What do you think that boy will be'!"[25]

1 *Master Jesus* I.
2 "The Infancy Gospel of James". Quoted in *The Other Bible*, 390.
3 Ibid.
4 Ibid.
5 "A Latin Infancy Gospel: The Birth of Jesus". Quoted in *The Other Bible*, 405-406.
6 "The First Gospel of the Infancy of Jesus Christ", I: 19-20. Hone's *Apocryphal New Testament*.
7 Ibid., III:1-8
8 *Emmanuel's Book*, 43.
9 "The Infancy Gospel of Pseudo-Matthew: The Book about the Origin of Blessed Mary and the Childhood of the Savior". Quoted in *The Other Bible, 393-394.*
10 "The First Gospel of the Infancy of Jesus Christ", II: 5-10. Hone's *Apocryphal New Testament.*
11 *Aquarian Gospel*, 4:3-12.
12 "The First Gospel of the Infancy of Jesus Christ", VIII: 1-7. In Hone's *Apocryphal New Testament.*
13 Ibid. XIV:5-10.
14 "The Infancy Gospel of Thomas", Quoted in *The Other Bible*, 399.
15 Ibid. 400.
16 Ibid.
17 Ibid. 401.
18 Ibid.
19 Ibid. 402.
20 "The First Gospel of the Infancy of Jesus Christ", XV: 8-13. Hone's *Apocryphal New Testament.*
21 *Master Jesus I.*
22 *Aquarian Gospel*, 16:15-21.
23 Ibid. 16:1-14.
24 Ibid. 18:1-22.
25 "The First Gospel of the Infancy of Jesus Christ", XXI: 7-8. Hone's *Apocryphal New Testament.*

Chapter 4: India

The Indian sage and Jesus often met and talked about the needs of nations and of men; about the sacred doctrines, forms and rites best suited to the coming age.

Levi, *The Aquarian Gospel of Jesus the Christ*

Archangel Gabriel has made us aware, that when the Master Jesus traveled in the Himalayas he was known as Issa. Some writings refer to him as Saint Issa.

Many are the fascinating speculations on where Jesus spent 'the hidden years'. One account is given in a book called *The Unknown Life of Jesus Christ*, by Nicholas Notovich, which claims that high in the Himalayan mountains, in the Convent at Himis, there is a scroll written in Pali, which relates: 'When Issa [Jesus] was thirteen years old, the age at which an Israelite is expected to marry, the modest house of his industrious parents became a meeting-place of the rich and illustrious, who were anxious to have as a son-in-law the young Issa, who was already celebrated for the edifying discourses he made in the name of the All-Powerful. Then Issa secretly absented himself from his father's house; left Jerusalem, and, in a train of merchants, journeyed toward the Sindh (Sind), with the object of perfecting himself in the knowledge of the word of God and the study of the laws of the great Buddhas'.[1]

41

When I began studying the Bible, from the very beginning it seemed to me strange that Jesus lived with his family, worked with his father as a carpenter until he was about 30, then walked to the Jordan River to be baptized. He then lived an amazing life expressing boundless love, healing miraculously and teaching precepts that have lasted 2,000 years. One day, several years ago, I asked a clergyman about this, and he said, "It doesn't matter." Doesn't matter? In Scripture his birth is detailed with every action of all the people involved (not to mention the creatures) – his parents, the innkeeper, the shepherds and the magi. Much is written about what he said, to whom he said it and where he said it. His arrest and trial are detailed, as well as testimony for and against him. The Bible tells us of the bickering between the Jews and Romans about his punishment and who was going to take responsibility for it. We've also read in Scripture of his struggle with bearing the cross to Calvary and details of his crucifixion, death and resurrection. And yet, for approximately 18 years, he worked as a carpenter in Nazareth, with no mention of his words, actions or effect on others?

Then, in the '80s I discovered *The Aquarian Gospel of Jesus the Christ.* It offers an explanation of those eighteen years. I asked Archangel Gabriel if that book was authentic. He said it is. Jesus traveled all over the known world, learning and teaching as he went. In the same manner as he spent the last years of his life, he was followed ardently by many and rebuffed by the political rulers in those countries. Then I found other books that referred to Jesus and his travels. Thus, I bring together these writings to present a plausible explanation of those years.

> It is not certain what route Jesus took on his journey to the East. Here is one possible itinerary [shown by a map on pages 342-343 of *The Lost Years of Jesus.* Reproduced on last page by permission of Summit University Press.] via ancient roads and trade routes, reconstructed from the Notovich, Abhedananda, and Roerich texts and legends: Jesus departed Jerusalem . . . took the Silk

Road to Bactra, headed south to Kabul, crossed the Punjab and proceeded to a Jain area on the Kathiawar peninsula where Jain temples were later built near the town of Palitana. He crossed India to Juggernaut (Puri), made trips to Rajagriha (Rajgir), Benares, and other holy cities and, fleeing his enemies, went to Kapilavastu – birthplace of Gautama Buddha. Jesus took a trail just west of Mt. Everest to Lhasa (where the palace of the Dalai Lama was built in the 17th century). On the return trip . . .he took the caravan route to Leh, went south to the state of Rajputana and then north to Kabul. He proceeded on the southern trade route through Persia where Zoroastrian priests abandoned him to wild beasts. Jesus survived and arrived unharmed in Jerusalem.[2]

We will now begin with Jesus' journey to Eastern India, beginning with the story of an Indian prince who traveled to Nazareth and asked Jesus' parents if the boy could accompany him back to his palace for learning.

A royal prince of India, Ravanna of Orissa in the south, was at the Jewish feast [in Jerusalem].

Ravanna was a man of wealth; and he was just, and with a band of Brahmic priests sought wisdom in the West.

When Jesus stood among the Jewish priests and read and spoke, Ravanna heard and was amazed.

And when he asked who Jesus was, from whence he came and what he was, Chief Hillel said,

We call this child the Day Star from on high, for he has come to bring to men a light, the light of life; to lighten up the way of men and to redeem his people, Israel.

And Hillel told Ravanna all about the child; about the prophecies concerning him; about the wonders of the night when he was born; about the visit of the magian priests;

About the way in which he was protected from the wrath of evil men; about his flight to Egypt-land, and how he then was serving with his father as a carpenter in Nazareth.

Ravanna was entranced, and asked to know the way to Nazareth, that he might go and honor such a one as son of God.

And with his gorgeous train he journeyed on the way and came to Nazareth of Galilee. He found the object of his search engaged in building dwellings for the sons of men.

And when he first saw Jesus he was climbing up a twelve-step ladder, and he carried in his hands a compass, square and ax.

Ravanna said, All hail, most favored son of heaven!

And at the inn Ravanna made a feast for all the people of the town; and Jesus and his parents were the honored guests.

For certain days Ravanna was a guest in Joseph's home on Marmion Way; he sought to learn the secret of the wisdom of the son; but it was all too great for him.

And then he asked that he might be the patron of the child; might take him to the East where he could learn the wisdom of the Brahms.

And Jesus longed to go that he might learn; and after many days his parents gave consent.

Then, with proud heart, Ravanna with his train, began the journey towards the rising sun; and after many days they crossed the Sind, and reached the province of Orissa, and the palace of the prince.[3]

The following excerpt shows that Jesus always turned to ordinary people when he was teaching and healing, whether in other lands or in his own country.

The Encyclopedia of Religion tells us that Brahmins and Kshatriyas are considered the first and second of the three traditional, twice-born castes of India. The Vaisya is the third group or caste. Those not considered 'twice born' are the Sudras. "Lamas know that Christ, passing through India and Tibet, turned not to the Brahmins and the Kshatriyas, but to the Sudras – to the working and humbled ones. The writings of the lamas recall how Christ extolled woman – the Mother of the World. And lamas point out how Christ regarded the so-called miracles."[4]

Other sources suggest that Jesus traveled to India, as shown in this excerpt:

"There have been distinct glimpses about a second visit of Christ to Egypt. But why is it incredible that after that, he could have been in India?"[5] Some resources indicate Jesus' exact age when he visited certain countries and others do not. As a young teenager, we find him near the Sind, in India:

"In the course of his fourteenth year, the young Issa, blessed of God, came on this side of Sind and established himself among the Aryas in the land beloved of God.

"Fame spread the reputation of this marvelous child throughout the length of northern Sind, and when he crossed the country of the five rivers and the Rajputana, the devotees of the god Jaine [Jain] prayed him to dwell among them.

"But he left the erring worshippers of Jain and went to Juggernaut in the country of Orissa, where repose the mortal remains of Vyasa-Krishna and where the white priests of Brahma made him a joyous welcome.

"They taught him to read and understand the Vedas, to cure by aid of prayer, to teach, to explain the holy scriptures to the people, and to drive out evil spirits from the bodies of men, restoring unto them their sanity.

"He passed six years at Juggernaut, at Rajagriha, at Benares, and in the other holy cities. Everyone loved him, for Issa lived in peace with the Vaisyas and the Sudras, whom he instructed in the holy scriptures."[6]

Jesus was accepted as a pupil in The Temple of the Sun at Jagannath, where he learned the Vedas. His understanding of the laws amazed the Brahmic masters. One of the priests, Lamaas Bramas, loved the boy and one day asked him to define truth.

> "Truth is the only thing that changes not.

> "In all the world there are two things; the one is truth; the other falsehood is; and truth is that which is, and falsehood that which seems to be.

> "Now truth is aught (all), and has no cause, and yet it is the cause of everything.

> "Falsehood is naught, and yet it is the manifest of aught.

> "Whatever has been will be unmade; that which begins must end

> "All things that can be seen by human eyes are manifests of aught, are naught, and so must pass away.

> "The things we see are but reflexes just appearing, while the ethers vibrate so and so, and when conditions change they disappear.

> "The Holy Breath is truth; is that which was, and is, and evermore shall be; it cannot change nor pass away."[7]

This response fascinated Lamaas, and he proceeded to ask Jesus to define man. " . . . Man is the truth and falsehood strangely mixed. Man is the Breath made flesh; so truth and falsehood are conjoined in him; and then they strive, and naught goes down and man as truth abides." Jesus also described power, wisdom and faith. His definition of faith is given here: "Faith is the surety of the omnipotence of God and man; the certainty that man will reach deific life.

"Salvation is a ladder reaching from the heart of man to heart of God. It has three steps; Belief is first, and this is what man thinks, perhaps, is truth. And faith is next, and this is what man knows is truth. Fruition is the last, and this is man himself, the truth. Belief is lost in faith; and in fruition faith is lost; and man is saved when he has reached deific life; when he and God are one." [8]

Jesus and Lamaas went through the regions of Orissa and the Ganges valley. In Benares, Jesus learned the Hindu art of healing from Udraka, greatest of all the Hindu healers: the uses of waters and plants, heat and cold, sun and shade. He explained that the laws of nature are the laws of health and those who live according to these laws are never sick. One day Jesus asked the priests about their caste system. When they had related the various castes and their functions, Jesus said, "Then Parabrahm is not a God of justice and of right; for with his own strong hand he has exalted one and brought another low." And Jesus said no more to them, but looking up to heaven he said, "My Father-God who was, and is, and ever more shall be; who holds within thy hands the scales of justice and of right; Who in the boundlessness of love has made all men to equal be. The white, the black, the yellow and the red can look up in thy face and say, 'Our Father-God.' Thou Father of the human race, I praise thy name."[9]

The priests were all enraged at this, and planned to harm him, but Lamaas pled for Jesus' life and the priests drove him away with a scourge of cords. But the people heard him and loved his words; the concepts of the Brotherhood of Man and Fatherhood of God. Jesus taught by parables to the people, as he was to do later in Israel. Jesus was feasted in Behar, by a wealthy man named Ach and in Benares by Udraka. At Benares, a lawyer said, "I pray you, Jesus, tell who is this God you speak about; where are his priests, his temples and his shrines?" And Jesus said,

> The God I speak about is everywhere; he cannot be compassed with walls, nor hedged about with bounds of any kind.
>
> All people worship God, the One; but all the people see him not alike.

This universal God is wisdom, will and love.

All men see not the Triune God. One sees him as the God of might; another as the God of thought; another as the God of love.

A man's ideal is his God, and so, as man unfolds, his God unfolds. Man's God today, tomorrow is not God.

The nations of the earth see God from different points of view, and so he does not seem the same to every one.

Man names the part of God he sees, and this to him is all of God; and every nation sees a part of God, and every nation has a name for God.

You Brahmans call him Parabrahm; in Egypt he is Thoth; and Zeus is his name in Greece; Jehovah is his Hebrew name; but everywhere he is the causeless Cause, the rootless Root from which all things have grown.

When men become afraid of God, and take him for a foe, they dress up other men in fancy garbs and call them priests,

And charge them to restrain the wrath of God by prayers; and when they fail to win his favor by their prayers, to buy him off with sacrifice of animal, or bird,

When man sees God as one with him, as Father-God, he needs no middle man, no priest to intercede;

He goes straight up to him and says, My Father-God! and then he lays his hand in God's own hand, and all is well.

And this is God. You are, each one, a priest, just for yourself; and sacrifice of blood God does not want. Just give your life in sacrificial service to the all of life, and God is pleased.[10]

1 *What the Great Religions Believe*, 131.
2 *The Lost Years of Jesus*, 342.
3 *Aquarian Gospel*, 21:1-17.
4 Grant, et al, *Himalaya*, 148. Quoted in *The Lost Years of Jesus*, 269.
5 Roerich, *Altai-Himalaya*, 89-90. Quoted in *The Lost Years of Jesus*, 269.
6 Notovich, "*The Unknown Life of Jesus Christ*", Chapter 5:1-5. Quoted in *The Lost Years of Jesus*, 197.
7 *Aquarian Gospel*, 22:1-10.
8 Ibid. 22:11-31.
9 Ibid. 24:14-18.
10 Ibid. 28:12-25.
11 Ibid. 30:5-20.
12 Ibid. 29:11-13.
13 Ibid. 31:23-24.

Chapter 5: Tibet, Assyria and Persia (Iran)

Let us hearken to the way in which, in the mountains of Tibet, they speak of Christ.
Prophet, *The Lost Years of Jesus*

In Elizabeth Clare Prophet's *The Lost Years of Jesus*, she tells of several travelers to the Himis Monastery in Ladak, about 25 miles from Leh:

Nicolas Notovich, a Russian journalist who visited Himis in 1887, published *The Unknown Life of Jesus Christ* (1894), which includes his own earlier translation from 'two large volumes with leaves yellowed by time' entitled *The Life of Saint Issa: Best of the Sons of Men*[1] .

Swami Abhedananda published a Bengali translation of the Himis manuscript in 1929, titled *In Kashmir And Tibet*. Nicholas Roerich, an artist who painted scenes of his first Asian Expedition, wrote three books about his travels: *Himalaya* (1926), *Heart of Asia* (1929) and *Altai-Himalaya: A Travel Diary* (1929).

George Roerich, Nicholas' son, who accompanied his father, wrote *Trails to Inmost Asia* in 1931.

In 1939 Elisabeth G. Caspari and her husband traveled to Himis with a religious leader Mrs. Clarence Gasque and was shown a set of parchments by a beaming lama, who said, "These books say your Jesus was here."[2]

William O. Douglas, The Chief Justice of the United States, went to Himis in 1951 and wrote *Beyond the Himalayas.*

In the late 1970s Edward F. Noack and his wife Helen made a trip to Himis. Mr. Noack was a fellow of the Royal Geographical Society and the California Academy of Sciences. He wrote *Amidst Ice and Nomads in High Asia.*

In these modern times, it is difficult to believe that there are writings about Jesus, which have not been made known to the world, for whatever reason. But fortunately, there have been those courageous, curious individuals who traveled to the Himalayas across treacherous terrain to learn the truth about Jesus' travels, and then to write about it. In the monastery at Himis Jesus was known as Saint Issa. Archangel Gabriel confirmed this fact and in *'The Divine Plan'* (July 1996) told us that there are other written records in the world, which have not yet been found. He also told us that all Scriptural references to Jesus' love of and attention to women were purged by that male-dominant society, which also described Mary Magdalene as a prostitute, which she never was. Rather, she was very close to Jesus and traveled with him. Jesus' deep respect for womankind is expressed in this passage from *The Life of Saint Issa:*

> Then Issa said, Reverence woman, mother of the universe. In her lies the truth of creation. She is the foundation of all that is good and beautiful. She is the source of life and death. Upon her lies the life of man, because she is the succor of his labors. She gives birth to you in travail, she watches over your growth. Until her very death you bring anguish to her. Bless her. Honor her. She is your only friend and sustenance upon earth. Reverence her. Defend her. Love your wives and honor them, because tomorrow they shall be mothers, and later – the mothers of the human race. Their love ennobles man, soothes the embittered heart and tames the beast. Wife and mother – invaluable treasure. They are the adornments

of the universe. From them issues all which peoples the universe.

As light divides itself from darkness, so does womankind possess the gift to divide in man good intent from the thought of evil. Your noblest thoughts shall belong to woman. Gather from them thy moral strength, which you must possess to sustain your near ones. Do not humiliate her, for therein you will humiliate yourselves. And through this shall you lose the feeling of love without which naught exists upon earth. Bring reverence to thy wife and she shall defend you. And all which you will do to mother, to wife, to widow or to another woman in sorrow – that shall you also do for the Spirit.[3]

In 1935, Baird T. Spalding published a book, in six small volumes, about his travels in the Far East entitled *Life and Teachings of the Masters of the Far East*

The first four volumes will be recapitulated here. Volume V contains lectures given by Mr. Spalding the last two years of his life and a brief biographical sketch of him. Volume VI contains articles written by Spalding for *Mind Magazine*, 1935-1937, some of his manuscripts, including *Original of the Lord's Prayer*, and *Power of Thought*, as well as eulogies written by his friends.

In the Foreword of Volume I, the author states that he was one of a research party of eleven persons that visited the Far East in 1894. "During our stay – three and a half years – we contacted the Great Masters of the Himalayas, who aided us in the translation of the records. . . The Masters accept that Buddha represents the Way to Enlightenment, but they clearly set forth that Christ IS Enlightenment, or a state of consciousness for which we are all seeking – the Christ light of every individual; therefore, the light of every child that is born into the world."

Volume I relates their experiences during the first year of the expedition, when they met a master named Emil, who spoke of many things, such as Christ's birth: "This Holy Spirit, . . .

call this fourth dimension or what you wish, we call it God in expression through the Christ in us. It is in this way the Christ was born. Mary, the Great Mother, perceived the ideal; the ideal was held in mind, then conceived in the soil of her soul, held for a time there, then brought forth or born as the perfect Christ Child." (p.23) Note the term 'fourth dimension'. What could it mean? We live in a three-dimensional world, and yet in Scripture we find 'May be able to comprehend with all saints what is the breadth, and length, and depth, and height;' (Eph. 3:18) The fourth dimension, as noted in the beginning of the above quote, is the Holy Spirit.

Emil was a Master Teacher who accompanied Spalding's expedition in India and frequently quoted Jesus. He explained the meaning of Jesus' words. "When Jesus said, 'I am the door'; He meant that the I AM in each soul is the door through which the life, power, and substance of the great I AM, which is God, comes forth into expression through the individual." (p.38) Did not Jesus the Great Master say, ' . . . He that believeth on me, the works that I do shall he do also; and greater works than these shall he do; (John 14:12) Was it not Jesus' true mission here on earth to show that we, as Sons of God, or man in his true estate, can create as perfectly and as harmoniously as God does? When Jesus commanded the blind man to bathe his eyes in the pool at Siloam (John 9:6-7), was not this intended to open the eyes of all?

Spalding reports that his party witnessed many healings in the Healing Temple on their journey: "Some sufferers only walked through the temple and were healed. Others spent considerable time there . . . We saw one man, who was suffering from ossification, carried into the temple and completely healed. Inside of an hour he walked, completely restored . . . another man who had lost the fingers of his hand had them completely restored . . . Cases of blindness, deafness, leprosy and many other diseases were cured instantly . . . We were told that if the healing was not permanent and the infirmity returned, it was on account of the lack of the true spiritual realization of the individual." (pp.58-59)

Turning to Volume II, we find an example of Jesus' materialization as recently as the nineteenth century:

Our friend stopped talking, and all was deep silence for the space of about five minutes. Then the room lighted up with a brilliance that we had not seen before. We heard a voice. At first it seemed a long way off and indistinct. After our attention was attracted to it and our thoughts directed to it, the voice became very distinct and rang out in clear bell-like tones.

One of our party asked, 'Who is speaking?' Our Chief said, 'Please be silent. Our dear Master, Jesus, is speaking.' Then one of our friends said, 'You are right, Jesus speaks.'

Then the voice went on, 'When I said, "I am the way, the truth and the life," I did not intend to convey the thought to mankind that I, myself, was the only true light. "As many as are led by the Spirit of God, they are Sons of God." When I said, "I am the perfect Son, the only begotten Son of God in whom the Father is well pleased," I fully intended to convey the thought to all mankind that one of God's children saw, understood, and claimed his divinity; saw that he lived, moved, and had his being in God, the great Father-Mother Principle of all things; that seeing this, he then spoke forth the word that he was the Christ, the only begotten Son of God, and with true heart and steadfast purpose lived the life, becoming what he claimed to be. With his eyes fixed upon that ideal, he filled his whole body with that ideal, and the end sought was fulfilled.

The reason so many have not seen me is that they have put me upon a shrine and placed me in the unapproachable. They have surrounded me with miracles and mystery; and again, they have placed me far from the common people, whom I love dearly. I love them with a love that is unspeakable. I have not withdrawn from them; they have withdrawn from me. They have set up veils, walls and partitions, mediators, and images of myself and those so near and dear to me. They have surrounded us with myth and mystery until we seem so far removed from these dear ones that they do not know how to approach. They pray and supplicate my dear mother and those that surround me, and thus they hold us all in mortal thought. When truly, if they would know us as we are, they would and could shake our hands. If they would drop all superstition and creed and know us as we are, they could talk with us as you do. We are no different at any time than as you see us. How we would love to have the whole world know this. Then what an awakening, what a reunion, what a feast! (pp.14-15)

Further, from Volume II: "This is a new-age message to you, the same as it seemed to be a new-age message two thousand years ago. It is the same today as it was then; it is but the resurrection of the age-old message. This message was told thousands of centuries ago in language so simple that babes could read. The message is, that man of his own free will shall leave the man-made kingdom and evolve to the God Kingdom. The son of man is to realize his divinity, reveal this divinity in his body and affairs, and become the Christ of God in the Kingdom of God. 'Know ye not that ye are gods?'" (p.46)

In Scripture we find such statements also: "I have said, 'Ye are gods; and all of you are children of the most High'." (Psalm 82:6) "Jesus answered them, 'Is it not written in your law, I said, 'Ye are gods'?" (John 10:34)

Let us turn now to Volume III. Jesus here spoke of motivating thought, of how most people are "unconscious of the divine gift which is mankind's true inheritance". He spoke of "one primal element containing innumerable particles universally distributed, responding to vibratory influences, and all in perfect and absolute equilibrium or balance."

He said that scientists would come to recognize the presence of a power, which is now inactive only "because it is unrecognized." He spoke of the order of cosmic progression and of intelligent life. And then he said, "Spirit is primary, vibrating, originating power; and you may enter into spirit and use its power by the simple acceptance or knowing that it does exist; then let it come forth, and the whole of spirit is at your command. To you it becomes an ever-potent spring of perpetual and original life right within yourself . . . God is that power which is generated and exhilarated by your own thought action." (p.20-21)

And on page 38: "When the artist portrayed me at Gethsemane, the rays of light went out from my body instead of coming out from heaven to me. The light is the God-power generated from within my body, then sent out by the reflector. These beams go out from every body when that person stands forth as God in his divine heritage – the Christ of God ALL ONE."

Volume III contains many more teachings from the master Jesus, but a powerful prayer, which he gave to the Spalding expedition and translated into English, is the sum of what we shall present here to conclude this volume:

THE LIGHT

"As I stand alone in Your great silence, God my Father, in the midst of me there blazes a pure light and it fills every atom of my whole being with its great radiance. Life, Love, Strength, Purity, Beauty, Perfection, stand forth in all dominion within me. As I gaze into the very heart of this light, I see another light, – liquid, soft, golden-white and radiantly luminous, – absorbing, mothering and giving forth the caressing fire of the Greater Light.

"Now I know that I am God, and one with God's whole universe. I whisper to God my Father, and I am undisturbed.

STILL IN SILENCE

"Yet in this complete silence there exists God's Greatest Activity. Again I am undisturbed, and complete silence is all about me. Now the radiance of this light spreads to God's vast universe, and everywhere I know there is God's conscious life. Again I say fearlessly, I am God; I am silent and unafraid.

"I lift the Christ high within me and sing God's praise. In the tones of my music inspiration hums. Louder and louder within me the Great Mother sings of new life. Louder and clearer with each new day, inspiration is lifting my conscious thought until it is attuned to God's rhythm. Again I lift the Christ high and give close ear that I may hear the glad music. My keynote is harmony and the theme of my song is God, and God seals my song as Truth.

BEHOLD I AM BORN ANEW, A CHRIST IS HERE

"I am free with the great light of Your Spirit, God my Father. Your seal is placed upon my forehead. I accept.

I hold Your light high, God my Father. Again, I accept." (p.45)

In Tibet, Issa taught, saying: "Do not humiliate your neighbor. Help the poor. Sustain the feeble. Do evil to no one. Do not covet that which you do not possess, but which is possessed by others . . . Do not defile the nobility of your feelings . . . Raise up the fallen and sustain the hungry, succor the ailing, in order that you be entirely pure and just upon the last day which I am preparing for you." He taught the Holy Scriptures to the lower castes. "But the Brahmins and Kshatriyas told him that Brahma forbade those to approach who were created out of his womb and feet. The Vicias were allowed to listen to the Vedas only on holidays and the Sudras (peasants) were not only forbidden to be present at the reading of the Vedas but could not even look at them."[4] Jesus preached against their rulings and thus the priests and warriors plotted to put Jesus to death. He was warned by the Sudras and left by night for the Himalayan foothills in Nepal, birthplace of Buddha Sakyammi, five centuries earlier.

Jesus took a trail just west of Mt. Everest to Lhasa.[5] He traveled to Lassa (Lhasa), and stayed in the temple of Meng-tse, 'greatest sage of all the farther East', where Jesus and his host read the ancient scrolls of sacred wisdom together. Jesus did not teach in the temple, but he learned from Meng-tse.[6] He traveled to Leh in Ladak, teaching in many villages enroute. A woman who had heard of Jesus brought her dying infant to him for healing.

> "When Jesus saw her faith he lifted up his eyes to heaven and said,

> 'My Father-God, let power divine o'ershadow me, and let the Holy Breath fill full this child that it may live.'

> "And in the presence of the multitude he laid his hand upon the child and said,

> 'Good woman you are blest; your faith has saved your son.' And then the child was well."[7]

He taught the Ladaks how to heal, how sins are blotted out and how to make on earth a heaven of joy. When he left Ladak he said, "I go my way, but we will meet again; for in my Fatherland is room for all; I will prepare a place for you".

"And Jesus raised his hand in silent benediction; and went his way."[8] He left the Himalayas and journeyed west, preaching against idolatry along the way, and arrived at Lahore, Capital City of Punjab. He traveled with a caravan, on a well-outfitted camel that was a gift from merchantmen who had heard of his travels. Upon reaching Lahore he was greeted with delight by Ajainin and other priests. Ajainin was the priest who had come to Jesus in the night many months before, in Benares, to hear his words of truth. Jesus was Ajainin's guest and taught his host the secrets of the healing art, how to control the spirits of air, fire, water and the earth. He taught him also of the secret doctrine of forgiveness. One day as they sat on the porch of the temple, some traveling musicians paused before the court to sing and play.

Their music was most rich and delicate, and Jesus said, 'Among the high-bred people of the land we hear no sweeter music than that these uncouth children of the wilderness bring here to us.

From whence this talent and this power? In one short life they surely could not gain such grace of voice, such knowledge of the laws of harmony and tone.

Men call them prodigies. There are no prodigies. All things result from natural law.

These people are not young. A thousand years would not suffice to give them such divine expressiveness, and such purity of voice and touch.

Ten thousand years ago these people mastered harmony. In days of old they trod the busy thoroughfares of life, and caught the melody of birds, and played on harps of perfect form.

And they have come again to learn still other lessons from the varied notes of manifests.

These wandering people form a part of heaven's orchestra, and in the land of perfect things the very angels will delight to hear them play and sing'."[9]

PERSIA (IRAN)

On his way home to Nazareth Jesus traveled to Persia. He was not welcomed by the priests and ruling class, for he taught and healed the lower classes. They openly censured him, but he continued.[10] The neighboring countries resounded with the prophecies of Issa, and when he entered into Persia the priests became alarmed and forbade the inhabitants to listen to him.[11] He went to Persepolis, where the three wise men (Hor, Lun and Mer) lived, those who had brought him gold, frankincense and myrrh twenty-four years earlier. Matthew 2:11 describes that scene: . . . and when they had opened, their treasures they presented unto him gifts of gold and frankincense, and myrrh.

Knowing that Jesus was approaching the city, the wise men went to meet him. He told them of his travels and experiences. Three other wise men from the north came to see Jesus: Kaspar, Zara and Melzone. For seven days the seven masters sat in silence seeking light, revelation and power which would be required in the coming age. A feast was held in Persepolis. "And Jesus standing in the midst of all the people said, 'My brothers, sisters, children of our Father God; Most blest are you among the sons of men today, because you have such just conceptions of the Holy One and man. Your purity in worship and in life is pleasing unto God; and to your master, Zarathustra, praise is due.'"[12] Jesus explained to them the Silence, and how to enter it, and the rewards of listening in the Silence.[13] In Matthew 6:6 we find: But thou, when thou prayest, enter into thy closet, and when thou hast shut thy door, pray to thy Father which is in secret; and thy Father which seeth in secret shall reward thee openly.

Near Persepolis was a healing fountain where once a year, at a certain time, the blind, lame, deaf and dumb came to be healed. A little girl sat still as others rushed to the fountain and Jesus asked her why she sat and waited. She replied that, when all the others were finished, she could go into the water and stay as long as she liked. And Jesus said, "Behold a master soul! She came to earth to teach men the power of faith." And then he lifted up the child and said, "Why wait for anything? The very air we breathe is filled with balm of life. Breathe in this balm of life in faith and be made whole." The child breathed in the balm of life in faith, and she was well. [14] The Persian sages all said farewell to Jesus at the Euphrates River, pledging to meet him again in Egypt.[15]

ASSYRIA (Iraq, Syria, Jordan, Israel)

Arriving in Chaldea, 'cradle land of Israel', Jesus stayed for a while in Ur, where Abraham was born. And they went forth with them from Ur of Chaldees, to go into the land of Canaan; and they came unto Haran, and dwelt there. (Gen.11: 31) People came from far and near to hear Jesus. "He said to them, 'We all are kin. Two thousand years and more ago, our Father Abraham lived here in Ur, and then he worshipped God the One, and taught the people in these sacred groves.

'And he was greatly blessed; becoming father of the mighty hosts of Israel. Although so many years have passed since Abraham and Sarah walked these ways, a remnant of their kindred still abides in Ur. And in their hearts the God of Abraham is still adored, and faith and justice are the rocks on which they build'."[16] Ashbina, the greatest Assyrian sage, came forward and told the people that they were blessed by the presence of a prophet from God and he should be heard. Jesus preached of the brotherhood of man, the innate powers of humankind and the kingdom of the soul.

Jesus and Ashbina went together to the ruins of Babylon, walked the streets where Israel had been held captive.[17]

But after that our fathers had provoked the God of heaven unto wrath, he gave them into the hand of Nebuchadnezzar the king of Babylon, the Chaldean, who destroyed this house, and carried the people away into Babylon. (Ezra 5:12) Also, . . . Babylon is fallen, is fallen; and all the graven images of her gods he hath broken into the ground. (Isaiah 21:9).

They noted the willows where Judah's children had hung their harps, refusing to sing. In Psalm 137:1-3: By the rivers of Babylon, there we sat down, yea, we wept, when we remembered Zion. We hanged our harps upon the willows in the midst thereof. For there they that carried us away captive required of us a song; and they that wasted us required of us mirth, saying, Sing us one of the songs of Zion.

They saw where the Hebrews, with Daniel, stood as faithful witnesses. "And Jesus lifted up his hands and said, Behold the grandeur of the works of man!

"The king of Babylon destroyed the temple of the Lord in old Jerusalem; he burned the holy city; bound in chains my people and my kin, and brought them here as slaves.

"But retribution comes; for whatsoever men shall do to other men the righteous Judge will do to them."[18]

Jesus then went to Shinar and remained there seven days, and then he crossed the Jordan River and headed home to Nazareth. His mother greeted him with great joy and made a feast, inviting family and friends. But his brothers refused to attend, seeing Jesus as an adventurer, a worthless fortune hunter, returning after many years penniless. So Jesus talked only to his mother and his aunt, Miriam, about his journey, the lessons he learned and the works he did. "To others he told not the story of his life."[19]

1 Notovitch, *The Unknown Life of Jesus Christ.* Quoted in *The Lost Years of Jesus*, 11-16.

2 *The Lost Years of Jesus*, 312.

3 Notovitch, *The Unknown Life of Jesus Christ.* Quoted in *The Lost Years of Jesus*, 274-275.

4 *The Lost Years of Jesus*, 271.

5 Ibid. 342.

6 *Aquarian Gospel*, 36:1-10.

7 Ibid. 36:16-19.

8 Ibid. 36:35-36.

9 Ibid. 37:10-16.

10 Ibid. 38:1-5.

11 *The Unknown Life of Jesus Christ,* VIII: 1. Quoted in *The Lost Years of Jesus*, 204.

12 *Aquarian Gospel*, 39:3-5.

13 Ibid. 40:3-12.

14 Ibid. 41:14-21.

15 Ibid. 42:1-2.

16 Ibid. 42:5-8.

17 Ibid. 43:1-2.

18 Ibid. 43:5-7.

19 Ibid. 43:16-22.

Chapter 6: Greece and Egypt

Upon your brow I place this diadem, and in the Great Lodge of the heavens and earth you are THE CHRIST.

Levi, *Aquarian Gospel*

I was able to find only one source that described Jesus' travels to Greece and Egypt. The source is *The Aquarian Gospel of Jesus The Christ.* Therefore, all references are to the chapter and verse of that book. Jesus' journey to these countries is important because we hear Jesus' high praise for the accomplishment of the Greeks and their role in the history of humankind and in Egypt he entered the temple of the sacred brotherhood in Heliopolis for learning and acquired all the degrees essential for his spiritual growth, resulting in his being named The Christ.

"The Greek philosophy was full of pungent truth, and Jesus longed to study with the masters in the schools of Greece. And so he left his home in Nazareth and crossed the Carmel hills, and at the port took ship, and soon was in the Grecian capital." (44:1-2)

The Athenians had heard of Jesus as a teacher and philosopher. One of the Greek masters was Apollo, Defender of the Oracle. He was known far and wide as the Grecian sage. In the Aeropagus [amphitheater] Jesus heard many masters speak, but he knew he brought them a greater wisdom. He said,

"Of all the parts of earth there is no place more sensitized, more truly spirit-blest, than that where Athens stands. Yea, all of Greece is blest. No other land has been the homeland of such mighty men of thought as grace your scroll of fame." (44:11-12)

He reminded them that although Greece produced giants of philosophy, art and science, these disciplines were all steps on the way to worlds beyond the five senses. Intellect, he said, solves only problems of what we can see, but does not deal with reality and eternal law. He spoke of spirit-consciousness, which abides in every one but can only be awakened by Holy Breath, which must be called forth by the will of man. Purity, prayer and holy thought are necessary to let in Holy Breath. "Return, O mystic stream of Grecian thought, and mingle your clear waters with the flood of Spirit-life; and then the spirit consciousness will sleep no more, and man will know, and God will bless." (44:26)

The Grecian masters listened and accepted Jesus' words, although they did not all totally comprehend their meaning. One day as Jesus and Apollo walked on the seashore; a courier came and told Apollo that the Delphic Oracle wished to speak with him. Apollo invited Jesus to join him and they went to the Oracle. This is part of the message the Delphic Oracle gave to them:

"The Delphic sun has set; the Oracle will go into decline; the time is near when men will hear its voice no more. The gods will speak to man by man. The living Oracle now stands within these sacred groves; the Logos from on high has come. From henceforth will decrease my wisdom and my power; from henceforth will increase the wisdom and the power of him, Immanuel. Let all the masters stay; let every creature hear and honor him, Immanuel."(45:9-12)

One day as Jesus and Apollo sat together, Apollo asked Jesus if the Oracle was angel, man or a living god. "And Jesus said, It is not angel, man, nor god that speaks. It is the matchless wisdom of the master minds of Greece, united in a mastermind. This giant mind has taken to itself the substances of soul, and thinks, and hears, and speaks. It will remain a living soul while master- minds feed it with thought, with wisdom and with faith and hope. But when the master minds of Greece shall perish from the land, this giant master mind will cease to be, and then the Delphic Oracle will speak no more." (45:17-20)

This exemplifies for us the power of the mind of Man. When the focused thoughts of several people are combined, there is no limit to what can be accomplished. Archangel Gabriel presented a recent illustration of this group mind power during an early winter weekend seminar. The forecast was for stormy weather. Gabriel asked us what kind of weather we would like to have. So we discussed the matter and decided to ask for fifty-degree weather and no precipitation for the following day, when some of the seminar participants had to travel to New York City and New Jersey. We all concentrated together on that desire, picturing it in our minds. The next day was exactly what we had visualized. More than that – it remained that way for five days!

And in the Springwell Metaphysical Studies booklet "*Recognizing Your Power*", pp. 21-23 (11/7/97), Archangel Gabriel related another example of the power of this unified energy. He told of an incident in England during World War II.

> During your Second World War, England was under attack by the Germans. They were coming by water with a great battleship and submarines. They were coming by night and their intention was to invade England. They knew that England did not have a lot of defense in their own country because England's troops had been dispersed into other places in the world to fight the war.
>
> There was a group of psychics, mediums, and spiritual people who learned of this attack. The night that it was to take place, they gathered with their mops and brooms, for most of them were women. The men were off at war. There were elderly men and there were children, but most of them were women. They gathered together with their mops and their brooms and anything that looked like a rifle barrel. They gathered on the cliffs and along the edge of the

water and they prayed ardently and they chanted and they prayed and they chanted.

When the Germans came and they put up the periscopes from their submarines, in the gleam of the moonlight they saw what they thought was a great army. They saw weapons. They saw the shine of the moon on the barrels of rifles. The women had taken stovepipe and fitted it together and laid it over a rock and the Germans saw a canon. The Germans looked and they saw a great fortress well armed - thousands of men.

They radioed to one another; "We can't attack. They have prepared for us. We are only one battleship and five submarines against all of that. We had better withdraw." And they did. They never knew that the only things up on the cliffs were five or six hundred women with mops and brooms and stove pipes. Had they attacked by daylight, they would have seen, but they attacked at night.

The vibrations of the prayer and the chanting and the affirmative knowing that these people generated filled the ethers with a defense far greater than the German army could have ever overcome. What the Germans saw was not what was upon the earth but what was upon the ethers and England was saved. There have been many incidents upon your earth in which the unified energy of the spirit power has overcome adversity.

Recently, an English friend of mine told me that the above story is told in history books in England. Jesus makes it very clear, from the following story, that prayer and divine intent are not only desirable and effective, but we must realize this potential in ourselves, rather than expecting 'something out there' to save us.

"The next holy day, Jesus walked on the Athens beach. A storm came up and tossed the ships about. Many fishermen and sailors drowned. Jesus helped to rescue some and revive the survivors. The people on the beach, instead of trying to rescue those calling for help, gathered around altars with wooden idols, praying to the idols for help. When the storm subsided, Jesus admonished them for expecting help from weather-beaten forms of wood. He said powers from unseen worlds help only when man has done what he can and then can do no more. 'The most efficient prayer that men can offer to a god of any kind is helpfulness to those in need of help; for what you do for other men the Holy One will do for you. And thus God helps'." (46:17-18)

Before leaving Greece, Jesus gave an inspiring message to the crowd that gathered to bid him farewell on his journey to Egypt. The reader need not be reminded of the accomplishments of the towering intellects that resided in ancient Greece, including the prose of Galen, the poetry of Homer, the drama of Aristophanes, and the philosophy of Socrates. Indeed, the list is extensive. It is significant that the Master Jesus also regarded them with respect and admiration, which he expressed in a farewell speech before sailing for Egypt. He also explained the relationship between intellect and spirit power.

> The son of man has been in many lands; has
> stood in temples of a multitude of foreign gods;
> has preached the gospel of good will and
> peace on earth to many people, tribes and
> tongues.

> Has been received with favor in a multitude of
> homes; but Greece is, of them all, the royal
> host.

> The breadth of Grecian thought; the depth of
> her philosophy; the height of her unselfish
> aspirations have well fitted her to be the
> champion of the cause of human liberty and
> right.

> The fates of war have subjugated Greece,
> because she trusted in the strength of flesh,
> and bone and intellect, forgetful of the spirit-life
> that binds a nation to its source of power,

But Greece will not forever sit within the darkness of the shadow-land as vassal of a foreign king.

Lift up your heads, you men of Greece; the time will come when Greece will breathe the ethers of the Holy Breath, and be a main spring of the spirit power of earth.

But God must be your shield, your buckler, and your tower of strength. Then, on the Cretan ship Mars, the Hebrew sage sailed for Egypt.

(46:20-26)

EGYPT

"There is a tradition that Jesus traveled and studied in Egypt and other foreign lands in the years between the time we see a brief glimpse of him as a boy of twelve, talking with the learned men of the Temple in his own land, and the beginning of his teachings." *What Jesus Taught in Secret*, p.12

Upon arriving in Egypt, he went immediately inland to Zoan, where Elihu and Salome lived. They had taught Mary, Jesus' mother, twenty-five years earlier in their sacred school. Jesus told them about his life, his journey, his meetings with the masters and the good reception he always received from the people. He stayed several days and then went to Heliopolis, city of the Sun [near where Cairo now stands], to seek admission to the temple of the sacred brotherhood in the Temple of The Sun.

He gained an audience with the council of the brotherhood. The hierophant asked him why, with all the wisdom he possessed, he would seek for more in the halls of men.

"And Jesus said, In every way of earth-life I would walk; in every hall of learning I would sit; the heights that any man has gained, these I would gain; What any man has suffered I would meet, that I may know the griefs, the disappointments and the sore temptations of my brother man; that I may know just how to succor those in need. I pray you, brothers, let me

73

go into your dismal crypts; and I would pass the hardest of your tests." So, Jesus was accepted. (47:12-15)

The hierophant took a scroll containing numbers and names from the wall and said, "The circle is the symbol of the perfect man, and seven is the number of the perfect man. The Logos is the perfect word; that which creates; that which destroys, and that which saves. This Hebrew master is the Logos of the Holy One, the Circle of the human race, the Seven of time. And in the record book the scribe wrote down, The Logos-Circle-Seven; and thus was Jesus known."

(48:2-5)

In taking the vow of what they called the secret brotherhood, Jesus had to pass seven tests, one at a time, and it probably goes without saying that he 'passed' them all. Each had a specific purpose and all aspects of each were carefully planned. After each test, Jesus was given a scroll bearing the name of the degree that he had completed. The first and the last tests will be described here.

The first brotherhood test: Sincerity. Jesus was guided to a dimly lit room for his first test, with the instruction: "No man can enter into light till he has found himself. Go forth and search till you have found your soul and then return." (48:"6) Jesus read the sacred texts provided and interpreted hieroglyphs on the walls. He was there many days until one night a priest of the temple came to him and told him the high priests were deceivers and would keep him there forever.

"And Jesus said, 'My brother, man, would you come here to teach deceit? Am I within these holy walls to learn the wiles of vile hypocrisy?' Nay, man, my Father scorns deceit, and I am here to do his will. Deceive these priests! Not while the sun shall shine. What I have said, that I have said; I will be true to them, to God, and to myself." (48:17-19)

Then the tempter left and Jesus was taken to the council of the brotherhood again. Not a word was spoken, but the hierophant placed his hand on Jesus' head and handed him a scroll that said, SINCERITY. (48:20-22) Then, one by one, Jesus was led through the next five tests. After each he received a scroll describing the degree he had attained.

They were *justice, faith, philanthropy, heroism* and *love divine.* (Ch. 49-53)

The seventh brotherhood test: Christhood. Then Jesus became a pupil of the hierophant himself, for the senior course of study; which included secrets of the mystic lore of Egypt, mysteries of life and death and the worlds beyond the circle of the sun. Finally, he was required to work in the Chamber of the Dead, to learn the ancient methods of preserving bodies from decay. While working there, one day a widow came in with carriers bearing her dead son, her only son. She wept profusely in her deep grief. Jesus consoled her and assured her that her son was not dead but rather had left his body behind to go on to other work, as all must do.

> Now, if you harbor grief, and give your sorrows vent they will grow greater every day. They will absorb your very life until at last you will be naught but grief, wet down with bitter tears.
>
> Instead of helping him you grieve your son by your deep grief. He seeks your solace now as he has ever done; is glad when you are glad; is saddened when you grieve.
>
> Go bury deep your woes, and smile at grief, and lose yourself in helping others dry their tears.
>
> With duty done comes happiness and joy; and gladness cheers the hearts of those who have passed on. (54:10-13)

There is a poignant story about a little girl that Jesus saw in the Chamber of the Dead. What impressed me about it was Jesus' homage to her and the fact that he met a child whose words expressed the very ideals which he came to exemplify: Other carriers came in, bearing the body of a woman and only one mourner following, a young girl. As the cortege approached the door of the Chamber, the girl saw a wounded bird. She went to it, picked it up and folded it to her breast and returned to the bier. Jesus had been watching her and asked her why she left the dead to save the bird.

The maiden said, "This lifeless body needs no help from me; but I can help while yet life is; my mother taught me this.

"My mother taught that grief and selfish love, and hopes and fears are but reflexes from the lower self;

"That what we sense are but small waves upon the rolling billows of a life.

"These all will pass away; they are unreal.

"Tears flow from hearts of flesh; the spirit never weeps; and I am longing for the day when I will walk in light, where tears are wiped away.

"My mother taught that all emotions are the sprays that rise from human loves, and hopes, and fears; that perfect bliss cannot be ours till we have conquered these."

And in the presence of that child did Jesus bow his head in reverence. He said,

"For days and months and years I've sought to learn this highest truth that man can learn on earth, and here a child, fresh brought to earth, has told it all in one short breath.

"No wonder David said, O Lord, our Lord, how excellent is thy name in all the earth!

Out of the mouths of babes and sucklings hast thou ordained strength."

And then he laid his hand upon the maiden's head, and said, "I'm sure the blessings of my Father-God will rest upon you, child, forevermore." (54:20-30)

When Jesus' work was done in the Chamber of the Dead, he was clothed in purple robes and taken before the hierophant, who said to him,

Upon your brow I place this diadem, and in the Great Lodge of the heavens and earth you are THE CHRIST.

something spurious, counterfeit, and untrustworthy. These fourteen apocryphal books of the Jews, although apparently much like the other books, were segregated into a sort of fine-print ghetto between the respectable Jews of the Old Testament and the not only respectable but also very special Christians of the New. No reason for it was given – at least, no understandable one. So the idea naturally prevailed that these books about the Maccabee brothers, and Susanna, Esther, Judith, Esdras, Baruch, Tobit and Manasses, and the wise sayings of Solomon and Jesus the Son of Sirach, were tabu, and not to be read.[1]

There are differences of opinion on what the apocryphal books are. The previous quotation mentions 14. There are other publications which list as many as twenty-four *other* books as *The Apocryphal Books of the New Testament*, including the most significant books mentioned in this work: I Infancy ("The First Gospel of the Infancy of Jesus Christ") and II Infancy ("Thomas's Gospel of the Infancy of Jesus Christ").

There is an interesting point made in the apocryphal Gospel of Philip: "The rulers thought that it was by their own power and will that they were doing what they did, but the holy spirit in secret was accomplishing everything through them as it wished. Truth, which existed since the beginning, is sown everywhere. And many see it being sown, but few are they who see it being reaped."[2]

An emerging picture of Jesus as a teacher and traveler is found in Potter's book *The Lost Years of Jesus Revealed*: "Careful study of the Essene Scrolls from the caves by the Salty Sea, confirmed by the Egyptian Gnostic codices from Nag- Hammadi, reveals him to have been not only well-versed in the knowledge and culture of Rome, Persia, Athens and Alexandria, a wide traveler and a great teacher, but also an original, independent thinker and a dedicated existential empiricist (in the midst of absolutists), ever deliberately seeking new truth by observation and experiment, even unto death."[3] This description reveals a human being that taught and learned as he traveled widely. He interacted with seers and paupers alike, as he journeyed the known world.

From page. 13 of Volume *II The Life and Teachings of the Masters of the Far East:*

> There is not a character in all your history that stands out as Jesus does. You count your time before and after his birth. He is idolized by a majority of your people, and that is where they err. Instead of the idol, he should be the ideal; instead of being made into a graven image, he should be real and living to you, for he actually lives today in the same body in which he was crucified. He lives and can talk to you just as he could before that event. The great error with so many is that they see his life ending in sorrow and death upon the cross, forgetting entirely that the greater portion of his life is that portion after the resurrection. He is able to teach and heal, today, far more than he ever did before. You can come into His presence at any time if you will. If you seek, you will find him. He is not a king who can intrude his presence upon you, but a mighty brother who stands ready always, to help you and to help the world. When he lived upon the mortal, earthly plane, he was able to reach but a few. Today he is able to reach all who will look to him.

In the New Testament we find no instance where Jesus told others to worship him. However, Strong' *Concordance of the Bible* lists eighteen times in which he clearly stated, "Follow me". Why would he say this to his *followers*? He must have intended it for all people, everywhere, for all time to come. Since Jesus often said to the multitudes 'follow me' and never did he say 'worship me', it is important to understand what the word 'worship' meant in Aramaic, the language Jesus spoke. Therefore, the following definition is given from Lamsa's *Gospel Light*. Lamsa was raised in the Aramaic tongue, the same language as Jesus:

> The Aramaic word *sagad*, worship, also means to bend or to kneel down. Easterners in greeting each other generally bow the head or bend down. When a ruler or holy man is greeted, the people kneel before him. "He worshipped Him" does not imply that he worshipped Jesus as one worshipped God. Such an act would have been regarded as sacrilegious and a breach of the first commandment in the eyes of the Jews and the man might have been stoned. But he knelt before him in token of homage and gratitude. This is also a sign of self-surrender and loyalty. The blind man (John 9:38) worshipped Jesus in acknowledgment of his divine power and in appreciation of his compassion on him in opening his eyes. He had no knowledge of the claims of Jesus nor was he interested in his teachings, but he was convinced by the miracle performed that he must be a holy man and one empowered by God. [4]

From Matthew 15:9, " . . . in vain do they worship me, teaching for doctrines the commandments of men" (also Mark 7:7). And from Matthew 4:10, "Thou shalt worship the Lord thy God, and him only shalt thou serve" (also in John 4:23 and Rev. 22:9). Thus it is clear that it is our task, our responsibility, to follow Jesus. In order to follow him, we must see him as a pattern, and several sources describe him as such: "And Jesus said, I come to be a pattern for the sons of men, and what I bid them do, that I must do . . ."[5]

The process of patterning ourselves after Jesus at this time and the realization that the process comes from within each of us, is clearly stated in the following segment from *The Voice Celestial*:

> "Fear not," he said, "it is the Father's will
> To give his kingdom to you and to fill
> Your life with love and joy and peace divine –
> Ask and receive, all that He hath is thine."

Absorb the consciousness of Christ, make thou
Of him the pattern of thy living now,
And, lo, thine inner life shall suddenly
Become aware that thou thyself art He.[6]

For so many centuries we have believed in a God 'out there, somewhere' who had to be appeased and begged to; who would punish us if we didn't do His bidding, that we find ourselves balking at the idea that we are spiritual beings housed in a physical form.

"The difficulty we have with the notion that God can manifest in fullness in a man, is perhaps our own inner resistance to the idea that we ourselves are spiritual beings, gods, who must one day come ourselves to full obedience to the law of love and the full manifestation of our oneness with God. The mission of Jesus was first to establish that pattern, that standard, that ideal, that concrete example in the consciousness of mankind and then to challenge us to measure up to it saying:

'Ye are gods, and all of you are children of the most High'."
John 10:34; Psalm 82:6[7]

Edgar Cayce, known as 'The Sleeping Prophet', addresses Christ as a pattern in reading 3528-1: "For the Master, Jesus, even the Christ, is the pattern for every man in the earth, whether he be Gentile or Jew, Parthenian or Greek. For all have the pattern, whether they call on that name or not; but there is no other name given under heaven whereby men may be saved from themselves."[8]

This concept of Jesus as a pattern is also described in a lovely and rhythmic verse in *The Voice Celestial*:

So the Spirit that was with them

And the life that never left them

Caused them to awake and listen

To the message of creation,

Caused them always to remember

That they too, had unseen pattern,

That they, too, had inner likeness,

That all mankind too has likeness

In the mind and heart of God,

Have identity with God.[9]

Edgar Cayce, through his readings, gave us a plethora of information about Jesus. He also provided an explanation of the difference between 'Jesus' and 'The Christ'.

> We find in the (Cayce) readings the expression, "Jesus who became the Christ," and the statement that "The Spirit of the Christ took up the life of the man Jesus." Apparently, in being fully obedient to the law, He became the Law. The messenger became the Message. The life, death, and resurrection were the completion of the project undertaken with the manifestation of Adam and Eve in the earth plane. With the coming of Adam, what had been made in the image of God, the souls of us all, had a temple in which to come to an awareness of that oneness while still in the earth plane. Next, the pattern of the image of God, written in all our souls, had to become lived out in the life of man. As Jesus fully lived out this pattern, He *became* the pattern and the ideal, the standard for us all. The Christ is the *power* – Jesus is the *pattern*.[10]

So many people have a problem with the idea that we can emulate Jesus the Christ. One reason is that too often we see ourselves as physical bodies, consciously (or unconsciously) walking a spiritual path that is difficult and challenging. But the truth of the matter is that we are spiritual beings clothed in soul and flesh, living in a three-dimensional world and seeing only that, believing ourselves to be only what we see in our mirrors. We believe we are what our religions have told us we are throughout the centuries. " . . .Your awareness of God is rather dim and shadowy and much plagued by what you were taught in the schools of the religions of your choice. Religion has nothing to do with the spirit world. Spirituality has everything to do with it. Religion is man's idea of what God is supposed to be, and spirituality is what God is and what God knows mankind to be."[11]

Furthermore, John 3:16 states: " For God so loved the world, that he gave his only begotten Son, that whosoever believeth in him should not perish, but have everlasting life." There are other places in the New Testament (Hebrews and I John) which refer to Jesus as 'the only begotten Son of God.' Archangel Gabriel informed us: " . . . In transcribing from Aramaic into Greek into Hebrew and all the other languages thereafter, certain words have different meanings . . . "The begotten son of the only God," was soon turned around to be, "The only begotten Son of God." . . . [We] all are begotten of God and so was Jesus. [12]

I would like to take the time here to explain the constant reference to 'Son of God.' As a woman and like many other women who attended seminars and lectures of Archangel Gabriel, we addressed the issue and Gabriel's answer was that we *all* are sons of God, but if the women were uncomfortable with the gender aspect, we could think of ourselves as *suns* of God. This seems perfectly logical, if we turn to John 12:36 and read: "While ye have light, believe in the light that ye may be the children of light . . ."

Jesus' birth and the place he took in the evolvement of the Christs (see Chapter Two) is addressed in the following excerpt: "The (Cayce) readings indicate that the spirit of Christ was with the Buddha in his meditations, that this Spirit manifested in the high priest, Melchizedek, and in the service aspects of Joshua. This same Christ Spirit *took up* the life of the man Jesus completely. Wherever there has been the teaching of the One God, the Spirit of the Christ has been present; and wherever there has been a need of mankind, He has been working. Thus, we are told in the Old Testament prophecy of His coming to be born in Bethlehem: 'Out of thee shall He come forth unto me that is to be the ruler in Israel; whose goings forth have been from the old, from everlasting.'   Micah 5:2.[13]

Christ's life symbolizes man's struggle for infinite possibilities.[14]

Archangel Gabriel described the scene at Jesus' baptism and its metaphysical significance:

> A dove appeared and a voice said, "This is my son in whom I am well pleased." The Christ energy was far beyond the realm of consciousness of Jesus but went into the soul properties of Jesus. Your scattered (thoughts of) love and wisdom are sheep called into the Fold (baptism). It is a washing away of all past states of consciousness. Now there is a oneness that would never be gone; a divine connection was made; Jesus was transformed – all past washed away. He needed to get used to it, to have this At-one-ment become an integral part of him. So he went into the desert alone and communed with angels and high masters until he could open this man in consciousness to the Christ with nothing in between; to truly become the Son of God. He was shown all details of his future, to rejoice and weep, to walk through the fears of it and come at last to inner peace. There is no Satan; it was his ego self.[15]

As he left the Jordan River, he realized that he had made a commitment. In his very being he knew 'the die was cast' and his path was a dedicated one. Finally, regarding Jesus' baptism, and perfectly in line with the title of this book, we present this illuminating phrase: "And as soon as Christ went down into the water he came out laughing at everything of this world . . . He who wants to enter the kingdom of heaven will attain it. If he despises everything of this world and scorns it as a trifle, he will come out laughing"[16]

Since Jesus displayed great wisdom as young as 12 years of age (in Scripture) and even as a baby in his crib (in the Apocrypha), we might wonder why he did not start preaching and teaching before he turned thirty. For some insight into this question, we find: "Western Biblical students, being unfamiliar with the customs and manners of the ancient Bible lands, fail to realize that in the Near East a young man under thirty years of age cannot sit in the council, nor can he teach law and religion. In that part of the world, one must be thirty years of age, well matured, to be accepted as a teacher of religion, a counselor, or an elder. Regardless of how brilliant a young man may be, until he reaches the age of thirty he is not respected as a teacher."[17]

In the book *The Voice Celestial* by Ernest Holmes and his brother Fenwicke (both ministers of New Thought churches and authors in their own right) we find this description of Jesus as a teacher of simple truths and powerful mien:

> Thus early was the Teacher brought to face
>
> The great enigma, and by what means to trace
>
> The doctrine of the soul, the what and why
>
> Of life and how is man to live and how to die.
>
> Yet it took time, for though he had attained
>
> Such powers of mind as seldom have been gained
>
> Or given men, or avatars or seers,
>
> Yet wisdom needs the ripening of years.
>
> But came the day which prophecy foretold
>
> In ev'ry land down from the ages old
>
> When "*He*" should come, the mightiest and best
>
> Of all the seers by whom the earth was blessed.
>
> Not ushered in by thunder and by might
>
> Like Moses gleaming with celestial Light;
>
> But, dressed in simple robe with sandalled feet,
>
> He made a temple of the village street.[18]

This evokes a picture of Jesus, treading the streets and highways of his native land. We tend to draw a picture in our mind of his appearance. At a question and answer session on December 12, 1994, Archangel Gabriel was asked to describe the Master Jesus.

> The Master Jesus was a very powerfully built man. He worked very hard; he was well muscled. He was about six feet tall – slender, but broad-framed. His hair was a light brown with a lot of red lights through it. His eyes were very, very blue. He walked with a great purpose in his stride, because he was fearless. He also had a wondrous sense of humor and he laughed – a lot. He poked fun at his apostles, in a loving way. He sometimes taunted them into learning the truths that they didn't learn in his presenting them in another way. He loved children. He loved to play with the children – a game you call 'hide and seek'. He loved the creatures. Creatures found a great refuge in him; they could hide with him and he would protect them from their pursuers.
>
> He loved people, and he greeted them with a great deal of love, and always with humor. A lot of the healing he did he did by means of allowing the person to see the humor in a situation; therefore laugh at it, and in laughing cast off a negative vibration thereof. The people who followed him followed him not because he was solemn and taught deep truths; but because he was light, materially and figuratively. He laughed; he taught them to laugh. He played games with them. He admired openly the ladies. Everyone thinks of him as being very chaste and pious; he was far from either one. He entered into life with a deep and abiding love for life. He lived life lovingly. He had his moods; sometimes he wanted to be alone just to go within himself; and there were times he could chase off a most ardent follower, by simply turning and

looking at them [sic] and they would back off.
He had times of being very despondent,
especially when he would have taught all day;
for knowing that of the thousands who came to
hear, perhaps there were ten who understood.
He frequently questioned the wisdom of his
mission and often sought angel guidance and
help. Many times we were called upon simply
to come and sit with him, to comfort him, to
bolster him up; to remind him of who he was,
and why he had come. He missed his mother
when he was away from her, and frequently
sent couriers with messages for her. He
simply adored Joseph, regarded him with great
respect. He loved being with him and learning
from him. He never, at any point, put himself
above his parents. When he was in their
presence he was their servant. He treated the
men who worked with him with a great deal of
respect, but he also was not above dumping
them out of the boat in fun. He also taught in a
manner that they learned as much by
observing him as by what he said, and he
never, ever, blamed anyone for anything that
happened to him – ever . . . His love was
complete.

Archangel Gabriel made it very clear that Jesus did not
come to start a new religion; that he was a good Jew and
knew well all the sacred scripture, quoting it often. In *History
of Religion* we find: "The religion of Jesus, therefore, is one
of love alone . . . His life is a demonstration, in every detail,
of the effects of his religion; all flows with the utmost
simplicity, and even as a matter of necessity, out of the truth
he taught. What he preached was, in fact, himself; he was
himself living in the kingdom of God, to which he called
others to come . . . he saw with perfect clearness what men
must be, and on what terms they must live together when
God and they were as Father and children to each other.
What he thus knew he lived, as if no laws but those of the
kingdom of heaven had any authority for him."[19] Later, in the
same book: "This . . . is the immediate and native tendency

of the religion of Jesus; it opens the prison doors to them that are bound; it communicates by its inner encouragement an energy which makes the infirm forget their weaknesses, it fills the heart with hope and opens up new views of what man can do and can become."[20]

Emmanuel's Book vividly describes Jesus' continuing mission and place in our lives at this time:

Who was Jesus Christ?

Christ is a teacher.

I say 'is', not 'was'

for He still exists

and is very much available

to all of you here.

He is a Spirit of Love and Light,

of brotherhood and healing.

He is deeply involved

with the human world.

Jesus is my brother.

Your brother, as well.

A Being of Light.

There is not one person

who enters this physical world

who is not, at the core,

a Being of Light.

Jesus Christ

is the supreme example

of the reality of Light

in the human world.[21]

The mighty teacher that he was " . . . lived in a world of spiritual realization far beyond that of which the average man has any understanding. As spiritual things must be spiritually discerned, so the full meaning of his sayings can never be clear to us until we have attained a consciousness equal to his."[22] A consciousness equal to his would appear to many impossible. Until we take Jesus down off the pedestal of idolization and come to know him as a man who lived the Love in which he, like us, was created, it will be impossible.

One way we may be able to see Jesus as a brother, rather than an idol, is to picture him as Archangel Gabriel described him on May 1, 1998 in *I Am The Christ*, (pp.18-19):

> When the Master Jesus walked, he strode along. When he came to a bluff over the sea, he would say, "Look at that. Is that not glorious? Look at the handiwork of God." Others might say, "It is just water and sand!" But Jesus would say, "Wake up and look at what is before you. Look at the sky, not a cloud in the sky." This is the limitlessness of the human spirit. His lessons were moment to moment. He stopped and talked to the flowers. He loved the creatures. He could stand and hold a conversation with a camel for half an hour. Everything around him by his perception vibrated with the beauty and the life of God, that same God that dwelled in him, that same God that filled his being.
>
> He noticed everything because everything was an expression of God to him. He enjoyed playing with the children. He enjoyed his moments of silence. Even when he would sit upon a hill with the sheep nearby and contemplate the stars, there was a sense of Godness with him.

In the marketplace surrounded by the throngs of people coming and going and the money mongers and all that sort of thing, there was still with him this awareness. "These are the children of God. These are my brothers and sisters. They don't know God is in them." He frequently would go up and address a person, "Hello, son of God," and he would get strange looks. But nonetheless he never lost contact with that knowing of the presence of God.

The victory at Calvary was not the crucifixion, but the resurrection. He came to show us that we are eternal and yet we turn our back on that idea in the sad belief that we are 'not worthy' to return to the Kingdom of God (which we never left, except in our limited awareness). We must give up the notion, which permeates society, that we are helpless victims of circumstance, and we must take full responsibility for everything and everyone in our lives.

Other prophets spoke in different modes

but Jesus spoke through the human experience.

Human experience was wedded to the spirit.

The lesson was lived and shown.

Christ was saying, "Look, humanity.

Look at what you can do.

See *who you are*."[23]

In the following excerpt of one of the seminars on the Master Jesus, Archangel Gabriel referred to Jesus' past incarnation as Joshua and its relation to his ministry as Jesus: "As he went forth to teach, he realized the difficulty of putting into words his knowledge. He knew how needy the people were . . . he recognized faces of past women and children ('take no prisoners') . . . the multitudes were people who Joshua had slain. Here was redemptive life force . . . redeeming in truth what had been slain in error."[24]

As told in Scripture, Jesus taught in the context of the life of the people. He spoke of shepherds and merchants and tax collectors. He was familiar with all experiences of the people he taught. He knew their lives were lived under the heel of Rome and that the Roman soldiers could have their way with them. It was a dark time to be alive. There were no freedoms, as we know them today.

All of His teaching is illustrated by the things of nature which reveal the glory of God and capture one's imagination. Moreover, He was intimately familiar with all the aspects of the life of the people – their business, their borrowing and lending, their dishonesty in buying and selling, their measuring with short or long measures and using diverse weights and crooked balances. He often saw partners in business, one with long arms who bought goods and the other with short arms who measured the goods and sold them to the people. This is why He says, 'With the measure with which you measure, it will be measured to you'."[25] Jesus did not just bring a teaching; he lived it. He understood that humanity had within it the same light that was within him; but over eons of time they had forgotten it. His task was to awaken them to what was already in them. "Part of the reason for the allusive and parabolic nature of his teachings lay in the fact that he was trying to induce in his hearers a new vision, a turning-around of their point of view. He was concerned with shaking people from their old categories, whether they were the sophisticated thought-patterns of the learned or the simple faith of the farmers, prostitutes, and fisher folk among whom he moved." [26]

In 1931 Charles A. Dinsmore wrote *The English Bible as Literature*. From the book's jacket I quote: "Dealing with elemental passions and principles, born of the genius of two remarkable races, modified by the influence of Greece and Rome, the final glory of our English Bible lies perhaps in its power to express itself . . . " Mr. Dinsmore addresses specifically the language Jesus used and the way he used it:

> We think of Jesus as a teacher, example, redeemer, but we are not accustomed to consider his marvelous power of literary expression . . . We call Jesus the Son of Man, humanity's 'realized ideal,' but in his mental processes he was a Hebrew of the Hebrews. He thought with a Hebrew brain and spoke

after the best manner of his people . . . He saw a truth and uttered it in clear, authoritative affirmations . . . he simply said: 'In my Father's house are many mansions . . . I go to prepare a place for you' . . . He spoke in metaphors and reasoned in parables . . . His sentences were clear, short, balanced . . . Jesus had the rare gift of so using common language that it glowed and became music; the hearers marveled at 'the words of grace that proceeded out of his mouth' . . . Jesus himself could say of them: 'The words that I speak unto you they are spirit and they are life.'

His words were on a level with his claims. He made assertions regarding his essential nature, his position in the course of the world's affairs, the responsibilities resting upon his shoulders, perfectly staggering in their audacity. There is in them no hollow ring of pretense, no bombast, no fustian. What impresses one reading the records is the ease and naturalness with which his words, weighty with truth and lustrous with beauty, fell from his lips. His words were as divine as his character. 'Never man spake like this man'.[27]

1 *The Lost Years of Jesus Revealed*, 49.
2 The Gospel of Philip, 55:5-20. Quoted in *Nag Hammadi Library*, 143.
3 *The Lost Years of Jesus Revealed*, 10.
4 *Gospel Light*, 363-364.
5 *Aquarian Gospel*, 64:7.
6 *The Voice Celestial*, 288.
7 *The Edgar Cayce Primer*, 222.
8 Ibid. 225.
9 *The Voice Celestial*, 282.
10 *The Edgar Cayce Primer*, 220.
11 Springwell, *States of Awareness*, 4.
12 Springwell, *The Christ Within*, 6.
13 *The Edgar Cayce primer*, 219.
14 *Emmanuel's Book*, 43.
15 *Master Jesus* I.
16 GPh II, 73.19, in NHL, p.144. Quoted in *Love Does Not Condemn*, 195.
17 *The Hidden Years of Jesus*, 26.
18 *The Voice Celestial*, 272.
19 *History of Religion*, 417.
20 Ibid. 424.
21 *Emmanuel's Book*, 42.
22 *Science of Mind*, 427.
23 *Emmanuel's Book*, 44.
24 *Master Jesus* I.
25 *The Hidden Years of Jesus*, 22-23.
26 *The Religious Experience of Mankind*, 319.
27 *The English Bible as Literature*, 277-279; John 7:46.

Chapter 8: His Ministry: In His Own Words

Do you believe that God would send you anything that is not
a blessing?   **Springwell, *Master Jesus III***

Jesus' teachings at home and abroad were consistent. He
explained to people everywhere that God is love, that we are
children of God but are not aware of it as he was aware of
his own At-one-ment. He gave a detailed description of God
in *The Life & Teachings of the Masters of the Far East:*

> Later the talk led to God, and one of our party
> said, "I would like to know who or what God
> really is." Then Jesus spoke, and said, "I
> believe that I understand the motive of the
> question you would like to clear up in your own
> mind. It is the many conflicting thoughts and
> ideas that are puzzling or disturbing the world
> today without reference to the origin of the
> word. God is the principle behind everything
> that exists today. The principle behind a thing
> is Spirit; and Spirit is Omnipotent,
> Omnipresent, Omniscient. God is the one
> Mind that is both the direct and the directing
> cause of all the good that we see about us.
> God is the source of all the true Love that holds
> or binds all forms together. God is impersonal
> principle. God is never personal except as He
> becomes to each individual a personal loving
> Father-Mother. To the individual He can be a

personal, loving, all-giving Father-Mother. God never becomes a great being located somewhere in the skies in a place called heaven, where He has a throne which He sits upon and judges people after they die; for God is the Life itself and that life never dies. That is but a misconception brought about by man's ignorant thinking, just as so many malformations have been brought about and you see them in the world around you. God is not a judge or a king who can intrude His presence upon you, or bring you before the bar of justice. God is a loving, all-giving Father-Mother, who, when you approach, puts out His arms and enfolds you. It does not matter who or what you are, or what you have been. You are His child just the same when you seek Him with a true heart and purpose. If you are the Prodigal Son who has turned his face from the Father's house and you are weary of the husks of life that you are feeding to the swine, you can again turn your face to the Father's house and be certain of a loving welcome. The feast ever awaits you there. The table is always spread, and when you do return, there will not be a reproach from a brother that has returned before you."[1]

In asking the question as to why Jesus came 2,000 years ago, we begin with Isaiah, proclaiming in the first verse of Chapter 61: "The Spirit of the Lord is upon me; because the Lord hath anointed me to preach good tidings unto the meek; he hath sent me to bind up the brokenhearted, to proclaim liberty to the captives, and the opening of the prison to them that are bound; To proclaim the acceptable year of the Lord . . ."

Centuries later, the man Jesus came, and in a synagogue in Nazareth, on a Sabbath day, he read those lines from Isaiah. . . . and he closed the book, and he gave it again to the minister, and sat down. And the eyes of all them that were in the synagogue were fastened on him. And he began to say to them, 'This day is this scripture fulfilled in your ears'. (Luke 4:20-21) Reflecting on his own appearance on earth,

"Jesus said: I took my stand in the midst of the world / and in flesh I appeared to them; / I found them all drunk, I found none / among them athirst. And my soul was afflicted / for the sons of men, because they are blind / in their heart and do not see / that empty they have come into the world / (and that) empty they seek to go out of the world again. / But now they are drunk. / When they have shaken off their wine, then will they repent." [2]

When Jesus returned from his travels to the Far East, he was asked by the elders, "Who art thou . . . we know not even thy name."

> "I am an Israelite," replied Issa. "From the day of my birth I saw the walls of Jerusalem, and I heard the weeping of my brothers reduced to slavery and the lamentations of my sisters who were carried away by the pagans.

> "And my soul was filled with sadness when I saw that my brethren had forgotten the true God. As a child, I left my father's house and went to dwell among other peoples.

> "But having heard that my brethren were suffering still greater tortures, I have come back to the country where my parents dwell to remind my brothers of the faith of their forefathers, which teaches us patience on earth to obtain perfect and sublime happiness in heaven."

> And the learned elders put him this question: "It is said that thou deniest the laws of Mossa (Moses) and that thou teachest the people to forsake the temple of God?"

> And Issa replied: "One cannot demolish that which has been given by our Heavenly Father, neither that which has been destroyed by sinners; but I have enjoined the purification of

97

the heart from all blemish, for it is the true temple of God.

"As to the laws of Mossa, I have endeavored to establish them in the hearts of men. And I say unto you that you do not understand their real meaning, for it is not vengeance but mercy that they teach; only the sense of these laws has been perverted."[3]

Centuries later Jesus, in more specific language, said this in a lecture entitled *The One*, p.24 (Springwell, December 3, 1995):

"You forget that you are sitting at the foot of the throne of God . . . But I know the truth about you. I know where you are, and that is why I come. I pray my Father knows how ardently I desire for you to know where you are. For long ago, I asked Him to please let you awaken, let you know that you are home."[4]

In the seminar titled *Master Jesus* III, Jesus gave a vivid commentary on his teachings 2,000 years ago:

> Much of what I taught on the earth has been greatly misconstrued and it has troubled me all this time. Much of the truth of it was left behind and it was molded and made into what mankind thought should be said. I have come in so many forms to people in so many ways to make right what was made wrong. Today I desire to straighten the crooked places so the truth of what I brought may be fully understood and lived and not bound by the old ways. (When I was on earth) it was a time when love was not expressed, not felt. And here comes this audacious, itinerant speaker who went out and clasped an arm around a friend, who liked to laugh; who enjoyed a good joke (if you don't think so, ask Peter).

> Within every human being there is a living Spirit that is the truth of your being and that Spirit is the child of God of you. That Spirit in you is pure and holy. It knows no sin, it knows

no error. It knows nothing of anything that would make you bad or wrong or not what you should be. That Spirit is cast perfectly; absolutely perfectly, in the image and likeness of God. Around that Spirit you have the personality that you yourselves have created and that personality is the Roman soldiers and the Hebrew people, if you will; the limitation, the bounds, the 'thou shalt nots'.

Humans have asked questions of me for 2,000 years: Did I exist? Was I indeed born of a virgin? Was God really my father and who was Joseph? And how could I be this man of sorrow, which I never was? I loved life. How can you love God and not love life? I spoke a truth and it resonates still because I spoke the voice of Christ. I spoke with the authority of my Father. Everything I did was because I was told to by the God within my breast – everything I did. Only a few of the words written about me were from the truth of the being of the writer – the others wrote what would be 'acceptable', what would be 'acceptable'.[5]

As we read the words of Jesus speaking of his Father, we recall Matthew 23:9: "And call no man your father upon the earth: for one is your Father, which is in heaven." Humanity is in dire need at this time of hearing the eternal truth of our own divinity – who we are and why we came and where we are going. The Master has always provided hope for the race of men, reminding us that after the dark of night comes dawn, and after our ignorance of who we really are, the light of truth will dawn upon our minds:

"And Issa said unto them: 'The human race perishes because of its lack of faith, for the darkness and the tempest have scattered the flocks of humanity and they have lost their shepherds.

"But the tempest will not last forever, and the darkness will not always obscure the light. The sky will become once more serene.

"The heavenly light will spread itself over the earth, and the flocks gone astray will gather around their shepherd.

"Do not strive to find straight paths in the darkness, lest ye fall into a pit; but gather together your remaining strength, support one another, place your confidence in your God, and wait till light appears'."[6]

The word 'light' has many definitions, including spiritual illumination, Inner Light, truth. Even comic strips, often use a light bulb to denote understanding. In *The Aquarian Gospel*, 52:11 Jesus gives a definition: " . . . but the breath of God vibrating in the rhythm of rapid thought." Thus, it is not surprising that the word 'light' appears nearly 300 times in Scripture. Here is a sampling: Isaiah 60:1, "Arise, shine; for thy light is come, and the glory of the Lord is risen upon thee." Proverbs 4:18, "But the path of the just is as the shining light, that shineth more and more unto the perfect day." Matthew 5:14, "Ye are the light of the world . . . Matthew 5:16, "Let your light so shine before men, that they may see your good works, and glorify your Father which is in heaven."

Jesus spoke of more than his mission and the kingdom of God. He also spoke of the planet earth and earthly power: "This, then, is not a material universe as you have thought; that is only your definition of it. It came forth from spirit, and it is spiritual if you will define it as such. This is orderly, true, basic. If orderly, it is scientific; if scientific, it is intelligent, it is life united with intelligent life. Life coupled to, and guided by intelligence, becomes volition; and through volition, it becomes vocation."[7]

But what has mankind done to this spiritual planet? Only a brief review of history reveals the plethora of wars and battles fought over land, boundaries and political power. Most people desire world peace, in which no generation ever again will send its sons and daughters off to war. When we think of world peace, do we think of a world at peace merely as a façade that covers underlying animosity? A peace where we 'look the other way' and try to ignore hatred and prejudice harbored by some of the population? Or do we seek a peace profound, which reveals at all levels a true and lasting peace between individuals and nations? It is fitting to ask this question, based on Jesus' comments about world peace:

> And Jesus said, "Peace reigns today; it is the peace of death.
>
> "A stagnant pool abides in peace. When waters cease to move they soon are ladened with the seeds of death; corruption dwells in every drop.
>
> "The living waters always leap and skip about like lambs in spring.
>
> "The nations are corrupt; they sleep within the arms of death and they must be aroused before it is too late.
>
> "In life we find antagonists at work. God sent me here to stir unto its depths the waters of the sea of life.
>
> "Peace follows strife; I come to slay this peace of death. The prince of peace must first be prince of strife.
>
> "This leaven of truth which I have brought to men will stir the demons up, and nations, cities, families will be at war within themselves . . .
>
> But right is king; and when the smoke is cleared away the nations will learn war no more; the Prince of Peace will come to reign."[8]

Would anyone not surmise that we are going through that strife now? All around the earth there are battles being waged within countries and between countries. One of the greatest phrases that President Franklin D. Roosevelt gave us during World War II was, "We have nothing to fear but fear itself." We must not only be fearless, but we must be able to discern truth from falsity, especially false gods. "Any false god will lead you from your path. Now, all truth lies within you. Great Masters come to point the way to your truth. Angels can only present to you what you have already in your consciousness for they merely strike a resounding chord within your own mind. Even though the information appears to you to be external, they draw from you, from your God, from your truth, from your Christ. They pull it forth, and they stand it in front of you, and they say, "Behold the truth." You look at that. You hear those words, and you say, "My angel told me thus and so." But all the angel told you is what you know, and Beloved Light, you know everything"[9]

We know everything – not all at once, of course, or we would be on overload, - but as we require to know something, it is there for our plucking from Divine Mind. Instead of being aware of that truth within us, we still look for a 'sign'.

The signs we seek are not visible, which Jesus makes very clear: "If the things that are visible to you are obscure to you, how can you hear about the things that are not visible? If the deeds of the truth that are visible in the world are difficult for you to perform, how indeed, then, shall you perform those that pertain to the exalted height and to the pleroma which are not visible?"[10]

Scripture tells that Jesus proclaimed himself king, said he had come as king. (John 18:37) However, he clarified this and distinguished between himself as Jesus the man, Christ the Essence of himself, and the king: Love.

> And Jesus, standing in the midst of them, exclaimed, "Behold, indeed, the king has come, but Jesus is not king. The kingdom truly is at hand; but men can see it not with carnal eyes; they cannot see the king upon the throne. This is the kingdom of the soul; its throne is not an earthly throne; its king is not a man . . . Men call me Christ, and God has recognized the name; but Christ is not a man. The Christ is universal love, and Love is king. This Jesus is but man who has been fitted by temptations overcome, by trials multiform, to be the temple through which Christ can manifest to men. Then hear, you men of Israel, hear! Look not upon the flesh; it is not king. Look to the Christ within, who shall be formed in every one of you, as he is formed in me."[11]

What I have found so enlightening in the ageless wisdom from Jesus and Archangel Gabriel is that we are not reaching for something we have never had or striving to become something we have never been. We have drawn away (in our consciousness only) from our source, which is God. Our task now is to return to that state of At-one-ment. This is clearly stated by Jesus in a lecture December 3, 1995:

> When you came forth into beingness, you were created in perfect peace. There was nothing in your creation excepting pure love, and nothing else to disturb. But as you became more confident of your individuality, you chose not to listen to the sacred voice within your heart, and you substituted fear for love. In that substitution, you created the very first and only error perception that you have ever made. All other error perceptions are merely fragments, pieces of this one error perception.
>
> For love is never substituted. Love is never changed. But you decided that fear was a greater god. So you followed the voice of fear, and you allowed it to rob you of the peace with which you were created. You allowed that error perception to overcome the light, and you believed that the light within you could be overcome. You believed in what you created, and you lost your belief in truth . . .
>
> Children, brethren, release and let go of your substitution and allow the truth of love and light to be your reality. You dwell in such shadows, and you call it reality. You have not seen reality in so long because you have clung desperately to its substitute, and you have believed that substitute to be the one God. You have not known God because you cannot know God and believe in evil. You cannot know God and experience hatred. You cannot know God and not call everyone your brother. For God is all of these things.

God is peace. The peace and the love and all
that God is, are within you. Only you, only you,
can open the door and cast off your
substitutions. For the Holy Spirit will take that
substitution and strip it of all that you have
made it to be, and you will see, and you will
know, and you will love and you will be the life
of which you were created.[12]

In *A Course in Miracles*, written by Jesus himself through a
dedicated scribe, we find in lesson 165: "The Thought of
God created you. It left you not, nor have you ever been
apart from it an instant. It belongs to you. By it you live. It is
your Source of life, holding you one with it, and everything is
one with you because it left you not. The Thought of God
protects you, cares for you, makes soft your resting place
and smooth your way, lighting your mind with happiness and
love. Eternity and everlasting life shine in your mind,
because the Thought of God has left you not, and still abides
with you."

It is essential that we know our source, and it indeed is
comforting to know that a loving, everlasting God is our
Source. Jesus gave us a proper response to those who ask
us about our source:

"Jesus said: If they say to you: / 'from where have you
originated?' say to them: / 'We have come from the Light, /
where the Light has originated through / itself. It [stood] /
and it revealed itself in their image'. / If they say to you:
'(Who) are you?' Say: / 'We are His sons and we are the
elect / of the Living Father.' If they ask you: / 'What is the
sign of your Father / in you?' say to them: 'It is a movement
and a / rest'."[13] In another text, "Jesus was asked, 'Who
taught you?'/ He answered, 'No one taught me. I saw that
the ignorance of the fool was shameful, so I avoided it.'"[14]

In *The Unknown Sayings of Jesus*, we find other interesting
comments made by the Master: One day Jesus was walking
with his followers and one of them said to him. "How is it
that you can walk on water and we cannot?" / He said to
them, "What do you think of the dinar and the dirham (pieces
of money)?" / They answered, "They are precious." / He
said, "But to me they are the same as mud."[15]

"Jesus said, 'This world is a bridge. Pass over it, but do not build your dwelling there'."[16]

Although there are many teachings of the Master in the New Testament, we find many more in other sources. We are reminded in John 21:25, "And there are also many other things which Jesus did, the which, if they should be written every one, I suppose that even the world itself could not contain the books that should be written. Amen."

Jesus did not spend long years working with his father as a carpenter, but he did spend some early years doing so. In *The Aquarian Gospel of Jesus the Christ,* Jesus gives us a detailed metaphysical description of the tools commonly used by a carpenter:

> These tools remind me of the ones we handle in the workshop of the mind where things are made of thought and where we build up character.
>
> We use the square to measure all our lines, to straighten out the crooked places of the way, and make the corners of our conduct square.
>
> We use the compass to draw circles round our passions and desires to keep them in the bounds of righteousness.
>
> We use the ax to cut away the knotty, useless and ungainly parts and make the character symmetrical.
>
> We use the hammer to drive home the truth, and pound it in until it is a part of every part.
>
> We use the plane to smooth the rough, uneven surfaces of joint, and block, and board that go to build the temple for the truth.
>
> The chisel, line, the plummet and the saw all have their uses in the workshop of the mind.
>
> And then this ladder with its trinity of steps, faith, hope and love; on it we climb up to the dome of purity in life.

And on the twelve-step ladder we ascend until
we reach the pinnacle of that which life is spent
to build – the Temple of Perfected Man.[17]

Jesus promised us in Scripture that the kingdom of heaven is within. Now he comes confirming that and tells us how to become *aware* of the kingdom which is within and thus is our birthright. Only through prayer and meditation can we hope to reach that kingdom in our awareness so that we, too, will become the Christ. "Jesus said: I will give you what / eye has not seen and what ear / has not heard and what hand has not touched / and (what) has not arisen in the heart / of man."[18]

Our senses have drawn us like a magnet from the truth of our being, which is light and love. We read that man is made in the likeness and image of God; yet man has created a god in his own image. Because we know wrath, we believe in a god of wrath. Because we seek revenge, we believe in a god of revenge. Because we are judgmental, we believe in a god who judges. With all of this negative thought and behavior, we are inclined to believe in the devil and that we will go to hell for our actions. However, during Baird T. Spalding's journey Jesus materialized many times to the party and at one time was asked where hell was and what the devil meant. "Jesus . . . said 'Hell or the devil has no abiding place except in man's mortal thought. Both of them are just wherever man places them. With your present enlightenment, can you place either in any geographical position on earth? If heaven is all and surrounds all, where could hell or the devil be placed ethereally? If God rules all and is ALL, where could either be placed in God's perfect plan'?" [19]

When I say to people that Jesus did not come to start a new religion, they usually quote Scripture: "And I say also unto thee, That thou art Peter, and upon this rock I will build my church; and the gates of hell shall not prevail against it." (Matt.16:18) Surely Peter was not going to be a physical rock; he was a symbol of the foundation of Jesus' teachings. Also note, "The stone which the builders rejected is become the head of the corner"(Matt 21:42, Mark 12:10, Luke20:17), referring to himself as symbol of his teachings, or the New

Testament which he would leave behind him. What Jesus meant was a belief system, not a denomination or sect. Note these Bible quotes: Acts 7:38: "This is he, that was in the church in the wilderness with the angel which spake to him in the mount Sinai, and with our fathers: who received the lively oracles to give unto us." Of course, a building would not be erected in the 'wilderness'. The New Testament is replete with phrases that use the word 'church' inferring a *belief* and not a building. In *The Way of the Essenes*, we find this express declaration from Jesus about the beginning of Christianity as a separate religion:

> I am not mouthing the terms of a blind, sanctimonious belief. I have not prepared you to receive the credo of a new faith based on a system that may be analyzed and taken to pieces. I am revealing to you the perception of the unique Essence, for everything exists beyond the duality of consciousness and words.

> Thus, when you speak in my name, I ask you not to establish a new religion. Your world has already known so many of them. They are all shadowed by their dogmas, as are cities by their walls. They forget that the Earth rumbles and that winds blow. Live and help others to live; feel and help others to feel; think and teach others to think. Do not impose what you know to be true, but help others to love the search for truth. People have always recited the thoughts of others. Let them, at last, recite their own thoughts that come from the deepest parts of their beings where they will see the light; where the Father – the Force – dwells; where they themselves dwell and always have. Thought is the essence of light, so let them learn to think.[20]

We are all lights of the world; we are all the 'only-begotten' of the one God. In our God-given free choice we have the option to seek to know our light and live it or to continue to pretend it isn't there. Too long have we been pretending.

Each of us must take the journey, in our own way, in our own time, guided by our own teachers. "You are one with Great Creative Mind Substance; thus you know that all things do exist. If you will but see that Divine Principle, Great Principle, Good Principle, God Principle . . . is all there is – that it fills all space, is all - then you are that principle; and as you stand forth in your Christ Dominion and give out this principle, you, by your very thought, word and act, give this principle greater activity. Thus one more has found his dominion and is using God Power and sending it out. As you give out this power, it flows to you. As you give, more is pressed upon you to give, and you will find you cannot deplete the supply."[21]

The ego, which is based on fear, shouts at us with a loud voice and only when we turn our attention to spiritual things do we open our inner ear to the still small voice of God. "And he said, Go forth, and stand upon the mount before the Lord. And, behold, the Lord passed by, and a great and strong wind rent the mountains, and brake in pieces the rocks before the Lord; but the Lord was not in the wind: and after the wind an earthquake; but the Lord was not in the earthquake: And after the earthquake a fire; but the Lord was not in the fire: and after the fire a still small voice." (I Kings 19:11-12) The ego and the Holy Spirit are differentiated in *A Course In Miracles*: "The Holy Spirit was given you with perfect impartiality, and only by recognizing Him impartially can you recognize Him at all. The ego is legion, but the Holy Spirit is one. No darkness abides anywhere in the Kingdom, but your part is only to allow no darkness to abide in your own mind. This alignment with light is unlimited, because it is in alignment with the light of the world. Each of us is the light of the world, and by joining our minds in this light we proclaim the Kingdom of God together and as one."[22]

Then the question becomes What can we do to become aware of this light within; when do we begin our conscious spiritual journey back to our origin, God? On the Spalding expedition, during one of Jesus' materializations he was asked, 'Can all bring forth the Christ?' He answered with a long discourse, only part of which is given here:

You must know that the hour you touch the deepest sorrow is the hour in which your greatest triumph begins. With all this you must know that sorrows can not touch you.

From that hour your voice will ring with a great, free song, for you fully know that you are the Christ, this light which is to shine among men and for men. Then you will know the darkness that is in every soul that cannot find a helping hand to clasp as he journeys on the rugged road before he finds the Christ within.

You must know that you are truly divine; and being divine, you must see that all men are as you are. You will know that there are dark places you must pass with the light that you are to carry to the highest, and your soul will ring out in praise that you can be of service to all men. Then with a glad free shout you mount to your very highest in your union with God.[23]

Humanity is on a path that spirals upward. As we take each step on our spiritual path, we are prepared for the next step. Although we may have days which seem dark, our spiritual journey is ever upward; we never have to start at square one again. As a race of God's children we are growing more concerned with each other, with our future generations and with the planet we call home, Mother Earth. As individuals and as groups joining together with a common purpose (growing into the awareness of what we truly are, spirit) our lights shine outward in all directions and attract other seekers. All the way Jesus is with us; accompanied by master teachers on the other side who join him. He said to the Spalding expedition to the Himalayas:

There are a great many of us joined together to help the whole world, and this is our lifework. There have been times when it has taken our combined energies to ward off the waves of evil thoughts, of doubt and disbelief and superstition, that have nearly engulfed mankind. You may call them evil forces if you wish. We know that they are evil only as man makes them so. But now we see the light growing brighter and brighter as the dear ones throw off the bonds. The throwing off of these bonds may for a time sink mankind into materiality; but even so, it is a step nearer the goal, for materiality does not hold one as superstition and myth and mystery hold one. When I stepped upon the water that day, do you think that I cast my eyes downward into the great depths, the material substance? No, I fastened my eyes steadfastly on God Power that transcends any power of the deep. The moment I did this the water became as firm as a rock and I could walk upon it in perfect safety.[24]

In John 14:12 we find the promise of the Master: "Verily, verily, I say unto you, He that believeth on me, the works that I do shall he do also; and greater works than these shall he do; because I go unto my Father."   And Jesus follows this up in *A Course in Miracles*, with:

There is nothing about me that you cannot attain. I have nothing that does not come from God. The difference between us now is that I have nothing else. This leaves me in a state which is only potential in you.

"No man cometh unto the Father but by me" does not mean that I am in any way separate or different from you except in time, and time does not really exist. The statement is more meaningful in terms of a vertical rather than a horizontal axis. You stand below me and I stand below God. In the process of "rising up," I am higher because without me the distance between God and man would be too great for you to encompass. I bridge the distance as an elder brother to you on the one hand and as a Son of God on the other. [25]

There have been philosophies regarding the existence of God. Is there a God? If so, what is God? And if there is a

God, why is the world in such a turmoil and why does He allow such negativity? How easy it is to lay at God's door all the ills of humanity on the one hand and, on the other, use our free choice moment by moment to create a world of our own. It is only in our free choice that we have created this turmoil. It is as foolish for us to question the existence of a God who created us, as it is for the ceramic bowl to question the existence of clay. "God's Word has promised that peace is possible here, and what He promises can hardly be impossible. But it is true that the world must be looked at differently, if His promises are to be accepted. What the world is, is but a fact. You cannot choose what this should be. But you can choose how you would see it. Indeed, you *must* choose this."[26]

The workbook in *A Course in Miracles* provides a daily guide for walking a conscious spiritual path. It is a personal journey back home to God for all of us prodigal sons. Whether we choose to take the path in this lifetime or another is our choice. But take it we must, all of us, to return unto our Great Creator. Jesus knew this well, and clearly stated it:

> Man came forth from God and he must return
> to God. That which from the heavens
> descended must again ascend unto heaven.
> The history of the Christ did not begin with my
> birth; neither did it end with the crucifixion. The
> Christ was when God created the first man in
> His own image and likeness . . . As God was
> his Father, so is He the father of all men, all
> are God's children. As the child has the quality
> of the parent, so the Christ is in every child.
> For many years the child lived and realized his
> Christhood, his oneness with God, through the
> Christ in himself. Then began the history of the
> Christ and you can trace this history back to
> man's beginning. That the Christ means more
> than the man Jesus, goes without
> contradiction. Had I not perceived this, I could
> not have brought forth the Christ. To me this is
> the pearl without price, the old wine in new

bottles, the truth which many others have brought forth, and thus have fulfilled the ideals that I have fulfilled and proved.[27]

Lastly, "The Lord said it well, 'Some have entered the kingdom of heaven laughing, and they have come out.'" (The Gnostic Gospel of Philip 74:24-27 as quoted in *The Other Bible*, p 88)

1 *The Life and Teachings of the Masters of the Far East*, Vol. II, 51-52.
2 *The Gospel According to Thomas*, Log.28, 19-21.
3 *"The Unknown Life of Jesus Christ"*. Quoted in *The Lost Years of Jesus*, 211-212.
4 Springwell, *The One*, 24.
5 *Master Jesus III*. (Rosendale, NY: Springwell, 1988), audiocassette.
6 *The Unknown Life of Jesus Christ*. Quoted in *The Lost Years of Jesus*, 210.
7 *Masters of the Far East*, Vol. III, 20.
8 *Aquarian Gospel*, 113:5-15.
9 Springwell, *The One*, 19.
10 "The Book of Thomas the Contender", II, 138:30-39. Quoted in *The Nag Hammadi Library*, 201.
11 *Aquarian Gospel*, 68:2-13.
12 Springwell, *The One*, 3-7.
13 *The Gospel According to Thomas*, Log 50,29.
14 *The Unknown Sayings of Jesus*, 150.
15 Ibid. Saying 198, 155.
16 *The Unknown Sayings of Jesus*, Saying 200, 156.
17 *Aquarian Gospel*, 20: 13-21.
18 *The Gospel According to Thomas*, Log. 17:5-9.
19 *Masters of the Far East*, Vol. II, 49.
20 *The Way of the Essenes*, 331-332.
21 *Masters of the Far East*, Vol. III, 21.
22 *A Course in Miracles*, Text, 91.

23 *Masters of the Far East*, Vol. II, 57.
24 Ibid. 53-54.
25 *A Course in Miracles*, Text p.5.
26 Ibid. Manual for Teachers, 28.
27 *Masters of the Far East,* Vol.II, 54-55.

Chapter 9: Crucifixion and Resurrection

> I am considered the Savior of the World. That is the
> biggest myth. I did not save the world – the world
> needs saving - if I had saved the world, your world it
> would not be as it is now, would it? There would not be
> murder and mayhem and war and men planning to
> send arms to kill a neighbor; people planning to bomb
> countries and take the physical lives of women,
> children and old people. If I had saved the world you
> wouldn't be in this room now; you would be the Christ .
> . . I didn't save anyone but myself.
> **Springwell, *Connecting to Your Source***

As explained in previous chapters, detailed accounts of
Jesus' experiences before, during, and after the crucifixion
are found in Scripture. Additional writings are here referred
to in order that the reader will have the benefit of other works
regarding these scenes, including apocryphal writings and
especially the information received from Archangel Gabriel.

In response to a letter from King Abgarus of Edessa, Jesus
wrote, in part, ". . . As to that part of your letter, which
relates to my giving you a visit, I must inform you, that I must
fulfill all the ends of my mission in this country, and after that
be received up again to him who sent me. But after my
ascension I will send one of my disciples, who will cure your
disease, and give life to you, and all that are with you." [1]

As we know, part of Jesus' mission was to go to Jerusalem
and be crucified. From infancy he knew what was coming; it

was part of his plan. Many times when Roman soldiers tried to grab him, he disappeared in the crowd. He 'disappeared' because he knew how to change the molecular structure of his body and take himself elsewhere. But when he had finished teaching the lessons he came to bring the world, he was ready to be crucified, and allowed his capture.

"Jesus told his disciples he was going to Jerusalem. They said, 'They will kill you'." Jesus knew he had to bring the message more profoundly. Scripture tells us that he rode into Jerusalem on a donkey. It was the way that Jesus could show humility; for a king to ride a donkey to his throne . . . He had let the Romans and the Jews at Qumran know 'I will ride a donkey.' His followers saw it as a suicide mission.[2]

There is a passage in the New Testament, when the multitudes were welcoming Jesus to Jerusalem on that first Palm Sunday, when the Pharisees said to him, "Master, rebuke thy disciples" (for all their noise). "And he answered and said unto them, 'I tell you that, if these should hold their peace, the stones would immediately cry out'."(Luke 19:40) Regarding inanimate objects having the capacity to express emotion, we find another interesting story in *The Apocryphal New Testament, Illustrated* (Nicodemus I:18-32): Pilate sent his messenger to bring Jesus to him:

> . . . as Jesus was going in by the ensigns, who carried the standards, the tops of them bowed down and worshipped Jesus.

> Whereupon the Jews exclaimed more vehemently against the ensigns.

> But Pilate said to the Jews, I know it is not pleasing to you that the tops of the standards did of themselves bow and worship Jesus; but why do ye exclaim against the ensigns, as if they had bowed and worshipped?

> They replied to Pilate, We saw the ensigns themselves bowing and worshipping Jesus.

> Then the governor called the ensigns and said unto them, Why did you do thus?

The ensigns said to Pilate, We are all pagans and worship the gods in temples; and how should we think anything about worshipping him? We only held the standards in our hands and they bowed themselves and worshipped him.

So Pilate ordered twelve of the strongest men to hold the standards and Pilate once again summoned Jesus to him. And when Jesus entered, the standards bowed as before.

Pilate and Jesus were both Essenes. Archangel Gabriel made that clear. Thus, Pilate cared about Jesus' safety and to that end summoned Jesus to him. Pilate told him of the dangers lurking all about Jerusalem and that the priests and scribes and Pharisees were stirring up the population against him. Pilate offered him a band of guards to see him across the border.

"And Jesus said, A noble prince has Caesar in his Pilate Pontius, and from the point of carnal man your words are seasoned with the wise man's salt; but from the point of Christ your words are foolishness. The coward flees when danger comes; but he who comes to seek and save the lost must give his life in willing sacrifice for those he comes to seek and save. Before the Pasch has been consumed, lo, all this nation will be cursed by shedding blood of innocence; and even now the murderers are at the door."[3]

Scripture tells us that Jesus was silent before Pilate, at the time of the trial, but actually he winked at Pilate, and Pilate sent everyone from the room. "'Why are you winking at me?' Jesus said, 'Condemn me.' Pilate said, 'I cannot.' And Jesus responded, 'Then get someone else'." But Pilate called the crowd back in, washed his hands and said, 'His blood is not on my soul.'"[4] Pilate had agreed to play his part in Jesus' mission before Pilate was born. Jesus had to remind him of that fact. He also had to remind Judas of his part in the crucifixion. The night before the Passover, Jesus called Judas aside and said,

"The time is at hand when you must do what you came to do." Judas said, "What did I come to do?" Jesus said, "To dip your hand in the bowl of deception and betray me." Judas: "I could not betray you." Judas had the most difficult task of all the disciples, for he loved Jesus . . . Judas wept . . and said, "I don't have the strength." . . . Jesus talked to him, and told him to ask for help from the angels . . . then he said, "Iscariot, on you rests the salvation of the consciousness in mankind. You must, so they will understand what I have taught . . . by not betraying me it is all for naught . . . because you love me, do this." Judas said, "I love you enough; if this is your bidding" – and Judas went forth and betrayed the man he loved.[5]

Right up to the end of his life, Jesus taught his disciples. In Massalian's orchard, before the scene in Gethsemane, Jesus gave a long message to them, and part of what he said is here given:

The Spirit of eternity is One unmanifest; and this is God the Father, God the Mother, God the Son in One

In life of manifests the One became the Three, and God the Father is the God of might; and God the Mother is omniscient God; and God the Son is love.

And God the Father is the power of heaven and earth; and God the Mother is the Holy Breath, the thought of heaven and earth; and God the Son, the only son, is Christ, and Christ is love.

I came as man to manifest this love to men.

As man I have been subject unto all the trials and temptations of the human race; but I have overcome the flesh, with all its passions and its appetites.

What I have done all men can do.

117

And I am now about to demonstrate the power
of man to conquer death; for every man is God
made flesh.[6]

When Archangel Gabriel was asked if Jesus suffered on the
cross, he answered, "No. Pain and suffering are the
greatest illusions of all."[7] Because humans are so
accustomed to pain and aches and suffering of all kinds, it
seems unfathomable that this could be so. But some
readers have probably heard of 'out of body experiences', in
which a person seems to be apart from their physical form,
observing it. Certainly this man who knew he was one with
God had such an ability. Gabriel related:

> When Jesus knew the crucifixion was coming
> he knew what he needed to do. But he
> questioned his ability . . . He knew he could not
> be in this [doubting] state of consciousness . . .
> Angels were told to leave him and observe only
> - it was the hardest thing we ever did . . . He
> reviewed his life. He remembered his baptism .
> . . Under the water where there was no . . .
> .earth sound, no breath; only God's spirit . . .
> out of the murky water into the clarity of light
> and the warmth of day . . . his awareness of
> "the die is cast". . . And saying "I am ready". . .
> (then) power came into him "I am the begotten
> Son of God." . . . He called in that Power and
> again it manifested in him . . . "The Father
> doeth the works." Thus Jesus grounded
> forever this consciousness as your reality.[8]

The New Testament provides great detail of Jesus' trial and
his sentencing to be crucified. The trial was over; Jesus had
been scourged, crowned with thorns, beaten. The time of
crucifixion had come. Simon, one of the Essenes, relates
this experience at the way of the cross (*The Way of the
Essenes*, 305-306):

"The custom was for any condemned person to walk all the
way from his cell to the place of execution, usually with his
hands chained. According to our information, the route was
traditionally the same, with death waiting beyond the walls
on a promontory that dominated the valley. Our role was to

locate the positions that a number of our people could occupy so as to be seen by the Master as he made his way, and to be able to help him if need be. By occupying key points, the Essenes who were among the one hundred and eight knew also that they could easily master the reactions and the movements of the crowd."

There is definitely comfort in knowing that there were supporters there for Jesus, as he trod the way of the cross; friends he could see as he went, standing among the crowd which jeered him. Another Essene, Daniel, described Jesus as he walked on the way and his emotional reaction to that historical, tragic scene:

> The Master's white robe had been ripped in countless places, and his body bore traces of many wounds that had dried stuck to the cloth. Upon seeing him appear at the corner of the street, the throng had been struck silent, amazed by the presence of the "Great White Rabbi" whom they had misunderstood and who, so close to his doom, still radiated such nobility. Everyone seemed petrified, trying to catch his gaze, which remained fastened on the ground. When the Master passed before us, he held himself straighter than ever, and seemed to smile at some invisible presence. It was then I saw that his face was bleeding, and that there were thorns tangled in his hair.

> The soldiers shoved us back against the stone post with grim determination, and we stood there frozen in dumb astonishment. I heard John bravely stifle a sob, heard him make a vain effort to breathe, to call to himself a bit of the life that was fleeing from us. Then he shuddered violently and broke out of the throng of people, running as fast as he could toward the porch. We watched him as he went away, and suddenly saw the Master from behind, his back streaming with blood. Then my eyes closed; at last they could close. My heart shut

its doors inward, full of a pain that an eternity, it seemed, would never be able to relieve.

For two thousand years now, my soul has been keeping the secret of these images, for two thousand years these sentences have been waiting, longing for expression at the tip of a pen, little chains of pointless words that could never really tell. . . .[9]

This story shows that the experiences that our soul's memory holds need to be expressed and resolved, or they will remain with us for several lifetimes.

Daniel continues, "The Master had still said nothing and was not even uttering the slightest cry of pain."[10] Knowing that Jesus did not suffer on the way to or on the cross, we have to ask how he did this. Archangel Gabriel explained that he stayed focused on the God-self of him, the Christ within which he knew was his At-one-ment with God. Thus, he could not interact with the noisy crowd in any way because it would have brought his consciousness into the earthly emotions that the crowd was expressing: anger, fear and hatred. As he focused on the Spirit self of him, he continued *even then* to heal, as the following stories illustrate:

1   [Years before] Jesus had seen a slave who had been flogged and left to die of thirst. Jesus got water for him, bathed him and brought him back to where he could live. When Jesus fell with the cross, that same slave was there and recognized Jesus' face and poured water on Jesus' head, and gave him to drink. Jesus looked at him and saw despair in his eyes. Jesus said, "Look behind you" and the man was thrown into the crowd by the soldiers. He looked behind him and saw his wife and children whom he had not seen for many years. . .

2   One of the soldiers who nailed Jesus to the cross had twin sons, one who suffered from epilepsy [a condition thought to be the inhabitancy of demons]. As he knelt to

nail, Jesus said, "In this hour thy son shall be healed." The soldier didn't understand, but when he returned home, his wife told him of the healing and when he asked his wife when it took place, he knew it was the same hour he had nailed Jesus. He was filled with great sorrow.[11]

We return to the scene at Calvary and Daniel's personal impression of the events taking place: "Meanwhile, the sky had curiously darkened . . . We could feel a slight wave of fear passing over the people who had remained. Then I saw that the legionaries were looking up at the sky, relaxing their surveillance.

"In no time, a thick blackness seemed to rise from out of the ground itself. It was like a sigh coming from the Earth . . . as if the Earth were trying to reach out, to get closer to the sky. The air became heavy, turning a dark gray."[12]

Now we find one of the most astonishing misinterpretations in Scripture. "And when the sun refused to shine and darkness came, the Lord exclaimed, *Heloi! Heloi! Lama Sabachthani?* Mark 15:34 interprets it to mean, My God, My God, Why has thou forsaken me? But Archangel Gabriel explained the similarity between 'God' and 'sun' in the original manuscript, and informed us that what Jesus really said was, O Sun, O Sun, why hast thou forsaken me? This is not difficult to understand by those who believe that Jesus could never question God nor assume that God had forsaken him.

Those familiar with Luke 23:44 are aware that it was very dark at the moment of the crucifixion: "And it was about the sixth hour, and there was a darkness over all the earth until the ninth hour. And the sun was darkened and the veil of the temple was rent in the midst." It was in this darkness that Jesus cried out to the Sun. Scripture doesn't mention that there was a last-minute stay of Jesus' execution as found in *The Way of the Essenes*:

> Lightning flashed and thunder rolled and a
> good many of those who had wanted to remain
> until the end fled wildly toward the ramparts . . .

The soldiers themselves had drawn off to one side to take cover from the violence of the rain. From their group finally emerged the man who, a few moments before, had arrived with what seemed to be a missive.

"Take your Master back, if there is still time," he cried, running toward some silhouettes streaming with water. "The emperor Tiberius has expressly ordered further investigation concerning him."

As he finished his sentence, he went up close to the Master, looked at him briefly, then declared, "I am sorry, it is too late."

He turned to the soldiers and cried to them, "You there! Finish off those two while they are unconscious!" (p. 316)

There is the suggestion of compassion here, when the Centurion ordered the two crucified men to be killed while they were unconscious. And in the midst of that tortured hour, one of the Essenes relates: "Around us we glimpsed wheeling forms, white and blue streaks, subtle tongues of gold and silver whirling over the valley. It seemed that all life in the flesh was being extinguished, and instinctively we felt like crying out – not in pain and fear of death – but in hope: a cry of victory! We felt strangely that everything was all right." (p. 315)

It is certainly refreshing to read of such hope at that dark time on earth. It encourages us to remember that no matter how dark life's experiences are, there is always something to be hopeful about, always a new dawning ahead. The Old Testament contains a detailed description of the crucifixion that would occur centuries later (Zechariah 12:10): "And I will pour upon the house of David, and upon the inhabitants of Jerusalem, the spirit of grace and of supplications: and they shall look upon me whom they have pierced. . . Also, as we turn to 13:6 of the same book, we find Jesus' comment about those who crucified him: "And one shall say unto him, What are these wounds in thine hands? Then he shall answer, Those with which I was wounded in the house of my friends."

For centuries, we have focused on the seeming suffering of Jesus, and have come to believe that sacrifice in any form is noble, even holy. But since Jesus did not suffer on the cross, we must now realize that it is time to focus on the glory of the resurrection and the eternalness of life rather than on the misery that the Master never suffered at all. "The Love of God surrounds His Son whom the god of crucifixion condemns. Teach not that I died in vain. Teach rather that I did not die by demonstrating that I live in you."[13]

This, and the following three quotes from the Text of *A Course in Miracles* define the real meaning of the crucifixion:

(1) "The crucifixion did not establish the Atonement; the resurrection did. Many sincere Christians have misunderstood this." (p.32)

(2) "I elected, for your sake and mine, to demonstrate that the most outrageous assault, as judged by the ego, does not matter. As the world judges these things, but not as God knows them, I was betrayed, abandoned, beaten, torn, and finally killed. It was clear that this was only because of the projection of others onto me, since I had not harmed anyone and had healed many." (p. 86)

(3) "The crucifixion cannot be shared because it is the symbol of projection, but the resurrection is the symbol of sharing because the reawakening of every Son of God is necessary to enable the Sonship to know its wholeness. Only this is knowledge.

"The message of the crucifixion is perfectly clear: '*Teach only love, for that is what you are*'." (p.87)

In contrast to the scriptural description of the scene at the tomb, we find the following amazing details in a lengthy explanation in *The Aquarian Gospel*, which explains specifically how the seal was broken and by whom:

> The tomb in which they laid the body of the Lord was in a garden, rich with flowers, the

garden of Siloam, and Joseph's home was near.

Before the watch began Caiaphas sent a company of priests out to the garden of Siloam that they might be assured that Jesus' body was within the tomb . . .

And Pilate sent his scribe who placed upon the stone the seal of Rome, in such a way that he who moved the stone would break the seal.

To break this Roman seal meant death to him who broke the seal.

The Jewish soldiers all were sworn to faithfulness; and then the watch began.

At midnight all was well, but suddenly the tomb became a blaze of light, and down the garden walk a troupe of white-clad soldiers marched in single file.

They came up to the tomb and marched and countermarched before the door.

The Jewish soldiers were alert; they thought the friends had come to steal the body of the Nazarene. The captain of the guard cried out to charge.

They charged; but not a white-clad soldier fell. They did not even stop; they marched and countermarched among the frightened men.

They stood upon the Roman seal; they did not speak; they unsheathed not their swords; it was the Silent Brotherhood.

The Jewish soldiers fled in fear; they fell upon the ground.

They stood apart until the white-clad soldiers marched away, and then the light about the tomb grew dim.

Then they returned; the stone was in its place; the seal was not disturbed, and they resumed their watch . . .[14]

The story continues, as the following night, at midnight, the Jewish soldiers heard a voice that said, *Adon Mashich Cumi*, which meant, Lord Christ arise. The soldiers unsheathed and drew their swords again. And then the words were heard again.

It seemed as though the voice was everywhere, and yet they saw no man. The soldiers blanched with fear, and still to flee meant death for cowardice, and so they stood and watched.

Again, and this was just before the sun arose, the heavens blazed with light, a distant thunder seemed to herald forth a coming storm;

And then the earth began to quake and in the rays of light they saw a form descend from heaven. They said, Behold an angel comes.

And then they heard again, *Adon Mashich Cumi.*

And then the white-robed form tramped on the Roman seal, and then he tore it into shreds; he took the mighty stone in hand as though it were a pebble from the brook, and cast it to the side.

And Jesus opened up his eyes and said All hail the rising sun! The coming of the day of righteousness!

And then he folded up his burial gown, his headbands and his coverings and laid them all aside. He rose, and for a moment stood beside the white-robed form. The weaker soldiers fell upon the ground, and hid their faces in their hands; the stronger stood and watched. They saw the body of the Nazarene transmute; they saw it change from mortal to immortal form, and then it disappeared. The soldiers heard a voice from somewhere; yea, from everywhere, it said Peace, peace on earth; good will to men.

They looked, the tomb was empty and the Lord had risen as he said.[15]

This explicit description is heartening to those of us who have yearned for the truth for so long. And so it was for Jesus' friends and followers. The news traveled fast when Mary Magdalene found the empty tomb. "He is risen" is a phrase we cannot say too often, for it proved beyond a doubt that life is eternal. This revelation is referred to in *The Formation of the Bible*, p.295:

"Two days after that fatal afternoon, extraordinary news suddenly spread among the circle of his friends: Jesus had *risen* from the dead! He had been seen and recognized. True enough, he had foretold the event, but it was, nonetheless, overwhelming. Furthermore, it was a revelation: what the Master had told his disciples had come to pass. And immediately they made the essential discovery – the discovery not only of the true messianic character of Christ, but also his transcendence, his divinity."

For centuries before Christ humans had acted on ancient stages the Passion Play, originating with the Eleusinian Mysteries in a Greek village called Eleusis. (*Encyclopedia of Religion*, p. 512) The theme of the play was that the hero died, went to some 'nether region' and reappeared a living entity. *The Voice Celestial* (p.325) provides us with a true perspective of that ancient drama and Jesus' resurrection:

"The greatest gift ever presented to mankind by seer, scientist or savior was made by Jesus – the demonstration and proof of a soul! Men had believed in a soul, they had taught their belief, they had fashioned 'Passion Plays' to illustrate it, but the final and definite proof lay in the teaching and experience of Jesus. There was only one way to prove it – to die and to reappear, not as part of a "play" . . . as in the Eleusinian Mysteries; but as an actual experience of death and survival." The following gives a succinct and apt description of Jesus' resurrection:

Behold ! The proof ! What all the seers had taught,

And what the Passion Plays sincerely sought

To demonstrate was brought at length to sight,

For Jesus rose and showed himself in light !

Untouched by death he broke at last the spell

That grips the common mind with fear of hell

Or feels the anguished torment of despair

Lest they shall see no more the face so fair

Of their beloved.[16]

A Course in Miracles constantly reminds us that what we see around us on the planet is all illusion. And in The Treatise on the Resurrection (Nag Hammadi Library, p.56): "Do not think the resurrection is an illusion. It is no illusion, but it is truth! Indeed, it is more fitting to say that the world is an illusion."

The seeming reality of the death of Jesus is clarified in the following poem that speaks of the eternality of life.

This the body that the Christ knew,

This the body that he spoke of,

This the body that was in him,

This the body he took with him,

On the mount of his transition,

On the dawn of resurrection,

On the day he left behind him

Nothing that man's eye could see.

For the pattern he brought with him

And his likeness in the unseen

Could not die nor be destroyed.

Only image of his pattern

Hung upon the cross of treason

Or was buried in the tomb.

The Voice Celestial, p.281

1"The Epistles of Jesus Christ and Abgarus King of Edessa", II:3. Quoted in Hone's *The Apocryphal New Testament*, 63.
2 *Master Jesus II.*
3 *Aquarian Gospel* 163:18-20.
4 *Master Jesus II.*
5 *Master Jesus I.*
6 *Aquarian Gospel*, 163:31-37.
7 *Master Jesus I.*
8 Ibid.
9 *The Way of the Essenes*, 309.
10 Ibid. 313.
11 *Master Jesus I.*
12 *The Way of the Essenes*, 315.
13 *A Course in Miracles*, Text, 193.
14 *Aquarian Gospel of Jesus the Christ*, 172:1-14.
15 Ibid. 172:25-42.
16 *The Voice Celestial*, 277.

Chapter 10: Materializations

How shall I tell the story
Of that life in whom the glory
Of the Father was transmuted
Into flesh and blood and brain
Of the Son of Man again?
Holmes, *The Voice Celestial*

The first four books of the New Testament all agree that the first person to see Jesus when he resurrected was Mary Magdalene. They also agree that he then appeared, materialized (in form of flesh) to all of his disciples. Scripture also describes his meeting with two disciples on their way back to their home in Emmaus, following the crucifixion. (Luke 24:13-31 and *Aquarian Gospel*, 174:1-23) These accounts will not be quoted here, as they are both rather lengthy. As we turn to other writings, we find many more instances of materialization. Jesus not only showed himself, but also spoke with many people in Jerusalem, Persepolis, India, Rome and Galilee. In retrospect, it seems fitting that he would do so, not only to confirm what he (and others) had prophesied about his resurrection, but also to revisit loved ones on the earth plane before ascending to heaven. Besides the materializations herein described, there is one passage in *The Apocryphal New Testament* in which others related they had observed his materialization, though they did not speak with him: "But a certain priest Phinees, Ada a schoolmaster, and a Levite, named Ageus, they three came from Galilee to Jerusalem, and told the chief priests and all who were in the synagogues, saying,

"We have seen Jesus, whom ye crucified, talking with his eleven disciples, and sitting in the midst of them in Mount Olivet, and saying to them, Go forth into the whole world, preach the Gospel to all nations, baptizing them in the name of the Father, and the Son, and the Holy Ghost; and whosoever shall believe and be baptized, shall be saved.

"And when he had said these things to his disciples, we saw him ascending up to heaven."[1]

As we know from Scripture, Jesus raised Lazarus from the dead after he had been entombed four days (John 11:48). He decided to visit Lazarus and his sisters again:

> Now, Mary, Martha, Ruth and Lazarus were in their home, and they had heard the rumor that their Lord had risen from the dead, and Martha said,
>
> It cannot be, for such a thing has never happened since the world began.
>
> But Mary said, Did not the Lord bring back our brother from the dead? and he could surely bring himself to life again.
>
> And as they talked, the Lord stood in their midst and said,
>
> All hail! For I am risen from the dead, first fruitage of the grave!
>
> And Martha ran and brought the chair in which the Lord had ever loved to sit, and Jesus sat down on the chair.
>
> And for a long, long time they talked about the trial, and the scenes of Calvary and of the garden of Siloam.
>
> Then Jesus said, Fear not, for I will be your boon companion all the way; and then he disappeared.[2]

As related in chapter four, when Jesus was thirteen he traveled to India with Ravanna, prince of Orissa, to study the wisdom of the Brahms. His visit as the resurrected teacher follows:

> Ravanna, prince of India, gave a feast. His palace in Orissa was the place where men of thought from the entire farther east were wont to meet.
>
> Ravanna was the prince with whom child Jesus went to India many years ago.
>
> The feast was made in honor of the wise men of the East.
>
> Among the guests were Meng-tse, Vidyapati and Lamaas.
>
> The wise men sat about the table talking of the needs of India and the world.
>
> The door unto the banquet hall was in the east; a vacant chair was at the table to the east.
>
> And as the wise men talked a stranger entered, unannounced, and raising up his hands in benediction said, All Hail!
>
> A halo rested on his head, and light, unlike the light of sun, filled all the room. The wise men rose and bowed their heads and said, All hail!
>
> And Jesus sat down in the vacant chair; and then the wise men knew it was the Hebrew prophet who had come.
>
> And Jesus said, Behold, for I am risen from the dead . . .This gospel of the resurrection of the dead is not confined to Jew and Greek; it is the heritage of every man of every time and clime; and I am here a demonstration of the power of man.
>
> Then he arose and pressed the hand of every man and of the royal host, and said,

Behold, I am not myth made of the fleeting winds, for I am flesh and bone and brawn; but I can cross the borderland at will.

And then they talked together there a long, long time. Then Jesus said,

I go my way, but you shall go to all the world and preach the gospel of the omnipotence of man, the power of truth, the resurrection of the dead;

He who believes this gospel of the son of man shall never die; the dead shall live again.

Then Jesus disappeared, but he had sown the seed. The words of life were spoken in Orissa, and all of India heard.[3]

Jesus then went to Persepolis, in Persia, to visit the three wise men that had brought him gold, frankincense and myrrh as a babe in Bethlehem. Now they were old men. It is likely that Jesus wanted to confirm their earlier expectations of a king coming to earth, and reveal the actuality of eternal life.

The magian priests were in the silence in Persepolis, and Kaspar, and the magian masters who were first to greet the child of promise in the shepherd's home in Bethlehem, were with the priests.

And Jesus came and sat with them; a crown of light was on his head.

And when the silence ended Kaspar said, A master from the royal council of the Silent Brotherhood is here; let us give praise.

And all the priests and masters stood and said, All hail! What message from the royal council do you bring?

And Jesus said, My brothers of the Silent Brotherhood, peace, peace on earth; good will to men!

The problem of the ages has been solved; a son of man has risen from the dead; has shown that human flesh can be transmuted into flesh divine.

Before the eyes of men this flesh in which I come to you was changed with speed of light from human flesh. And so I am the message that I bring to you.

To you I come, the first of all the race to be transmuted to the image of the AM.

What I have done, all men will do; and what I am, all men will be.

But Jesus said no more. In one short breath he told the story of his mission to the sons of men, and then he disappeared.[4]

Jesus also decided to go to the temple in Jerusalem, where the ruling Jews and priests who had sentenced him were now gathered on the Sabbath. But in this case, he appeared to them as a poor fisherman so they would not immediately recognize him. Among the group were Caiaphas and Annas.

A stranger came in garb of fisherman and asked, What has become of Jesus who is called the Christ? Is he not teaching in the temple now?

The Jews replied, That man from Galilee was crucified a week ago, because he was a dangerous man, a vile, seditious man.

The stranger asked, Where did you put the body of this man from Galilee? Where is his tomb?

The Jews replied, We do not know. His followers came at night and stole the body from the tomb in which it lay and carried it away, and then declared that he had risen from the dead.

The stranger asked, How do you know that his disciples stole the body from the tomb? Was anyone a witness of the theft?

The Jews replied, We had a hundred soldiers at the place, and every one of them declares that his disciples stole the body from the tomb.

The stranger asked, Will any one of all your hundred men stand forth and say, I saw the body stolen from the tomb?

The Jews replied, We do not know; these men are men of truth; we cannot doubt their word.

The stranger said, You priests and scribes and Pharisees hear me: I was a witness of the facts, was in the garden of Siloam, and stood among your hundred men.

And this I know, that not a man among your hundred men will say, I saw the body stolen from the tomb.

And I will testify before the God of heaven and earth, The body was not stolen from the tomb; the man from Galilee is risen from the dead.

And then the priests and scribes and Pharisees rushed up to seize the man and cast him out.

But instantly the fisherman became a radiant form of light, and priests and scribes and Pharisees fell back in deadly fear; they saw the man from Galilee.

And Jesus looked upon the frightened men and said, This is the body that you stoned beyond the city's gates and crucified on Calvary.

Behold my hands, my feet, my side and see the wounds the soldiers made.

If you believe that I am phantom made of air, come forth and handle me; ghosts do not carry flesh and bones.

> I came to earth to demonstrate the resurrection
> of the dead, the transmutation of the flesh of
> carnal man to flesh of man divine.
>
> Then Jesus raised his hands and said, Peace
> be to every one of you; good will to all
> mankind. And then he disappeared.[5]

Our term 'doubting Thomas' comes from the Bible story of Thomas, the apostle who doubted Jesus' resurrection: 'Except I shall see in his hands the print of the nails, and put my finger into the print of the nails, and thrust my hand into his side, I will not believe.' (John 20:24-28). This story is also told in *The Aquarian Gospel of Jesus the Christ*, 177:23-29.

Next, Jesus materialized in Greece, where years before Jesus had described the Delphic Oracle to Apollo and had reprimanded the people on Athens beach for worshipping a wooden idol rather than saving their neighbors caught in a storm at sea while fishing (see Chapter Six).

> Apollo, with the Silent Brotherhood of Greece,
> was sitting in a Delphian grove. The Oracle
> had spoken loud and long.
>
> The priests were in the sanctuary and as they
> looked the Oracle became a blaze of light; it
> seemed to be on fire, and all consumed.
>
> The priests were filled with fear. They said, A
> great disaster is to come; our gods are mad;
> they have destroyed our Oracle.
>
> But when the flames had spent themselves, a
> man stood on the orac pedestal and said,
>
> God speaks to man, not by an oracle of wood
> and gold, but by the voice of man.
>
> The gods have spoken to the Greeks, and
> kindred tongues, through images made by
> man; but God, the One, now speaks to man
> through Christ the only son, who was, and is
> and evermore will be.
>
> This Oracle shall fail; the Living Oracle of God,
> the One, will never fail.

Apollo knew the man who spoke; he knew it
was the Nazarene who once had taught the
wise men in the Acropolis and had rebuked the
idol worshippers upon the Athens beach;

And in a moment Jesus stood before Apollo
and the Silent Brotherhood, and said,

Behold, for I have risen from the dead with gifts
for men. I bring to you the title of your vast
estate.

All power in heaven and earth is mine; to you I
give all power in heaven and earth.

Go forth and teach the nations of the earth the
gospel of the resurrection of the dead and of
eternal life through Christ, the love of God
made manifest to men.

And then he clasped Apollo's hand and said,
My human flesh was changed to higher form
by love divine and I can manifest in flesh, or in
the higher planes of life, at will.

What I can do all men can do. Go preach the
gospel of the omnipotence of man.

Then Jesus disappeared; but Greece and
Crete and all the nations heard.[6]

In his materialized form, he also enabled others to perform
the miracle of walking on water. He appeared to a couple
who had befriended him in Galilee and had walked with him
on the shores of Galilee. They believed that he was the
Christ. The couple was in a small boat on the Tiber and a
storm from the sea wrecked the boat and they were both
drowning.

"And Jesus came and took them by the hands and said,
Claudas and Juliet, arise and walk with me upon the waves.
And they arose and walked with him upon the waves. A
thousand people saw the three walk on the waves, and saw
them reach the land, and they were all amazed."[7]

As so often happens in life, we visit places of our childhood
and we visit schools and colleges we once attended. And so

it is not difficult to imagine that Jesus would want to return to The Temple of the Sun in Egypt where he had passed all the tests to become the Christ.

> The priests of Heliopolis were in their temple met to celebrate the resurrection of their brother Nazarite; they knew that he had risen from the dead.
>
> The Nazarite appeared and stood upon a sacred pedestal on which no man had ever stood.
>
> This was an honor that had been reserved for him who first would demonstrate the resurrection of the dead. . . .
>
> When Jesus stood upon the sacred pedestal the masters stood and said, All hail! The great bells of the temple rang and all the temple was ablaze with light.
>
> And Jesus said, All honor to the masters of this Temple of the Sun.
>
> In flesh of man there is the essence of the resurrection of the dead. This essence, quickened by the Holy Breath, will raise the substance of the body to a higher tone.
>
> And make it like the substance of the bodies of the planes above, which human eyes cannot behold. . . .
>
> The masters looked; the form upon the sacred pedestal had gone, but every temple priest, and every living creature said, Praise God.[8]

Now we come to the time of Pentecost, which comes from the Greek *pentekoste*, meaning 'fiftieth day'. This was the day when the Holy Spirit descended upon the disciples. The Old Testament book of Joel, 2:28 promises, "And it shall come to pass afterward, that I will pour out my spirit upon all flesh; and your sons and your daughters shall prophesy, your old men shall dream dreams, your young men shall see visions. . . "

From the New Testament book of Acts, 2:1-4:

> And when the day of Pentecost was fully come,
> they were all with one accord in one place.
>
> And suddenly there came a sound from
> heaven as of a rushing mighty wind, and it
> filled all the house where they were sitting.
>
> And there appeared unto them cloven tongues
> like as of fire, and it sat upon each of them.
>
> And they were filled with the Holy Ghost, and
> began to speak with other tongues, as the
> Spirit gave them utterance.

As Jesus had requested, his followers had all gathered in Jerusalem. The following rendering, found in *The Aquarian Gospel*, is not unlike the Scripture verses:

> Now, when the day of Pentecost came
> Jerusalem was filled with pious Jews and
> proselytes from many lands.
>
> The Christines all were met and were in perfect
> harmony.
>
> And as they sat in silent prayer they heard a
> sound a-like the distant murmur of a coming
> storm.
>
> The sound grew loud, and louder still, until, like
> thunder peals, it filled the room where the
> apostles sat.
>
> A brilliant light appeared, and many thought,
> The building is afire.
>
> Twelve balls, that seemed like balls of fire, fell
> from heaven – a ball from every sign of all the
> circle of the heavens, and on the head of each
> apostle there appeared a flaming ball of fire.
>
> And every ball sent seven tongues of fire
> toward heaven, and each apostle spoke in
> seven dialects of earth.

The ignorant rabble treated lightly what they
heard and saw; they said, These men are
drunk, and know not what they say.

But men of learning were amazed; they said,
Are not these men who speak all Jews? How
is it that they speak in all the languages of
earth?"[9]

Archangel Gabriel told us: "The disciples were in a mental
space where you cannot argue; Jesus opened their
understanding (called 'wind'). So the disciples finally got
Jesus' message, it took three days. But, as often happens,
after a few days, they fell back to their old belief system."[10]
Even though the disciples were dedicated to the teachings of
Jesus, human frailty which we all are heirs to, prevailed and
soon after Pentecost they returned to their old belief
systems.

The final materialization of the Master at that time in history
is found in "The Secret Book of James":

And five hundred fifty days after he rose from the dead, we
said to him, "Did you depart and leave us?"

Jesus said, "No, but I shall return to the place from which I
have come. If you want to come with me, come."

They all answered and said, "If you order us, we shall come."

He said, "In truth I say to you, no one will ever enter
heaven's kingdom because I ordered it, but rather because
you yourselves are filled . . ."[11]

Jesus makes very clear to us that our spiritual growth and
our final ascension are personal responsibilities which each
of us must bear. His own ascension is described for us with
imagery of light, wholeness, and union with the Divine.

"And then they saw him rise upon the wings of light; a wreath encircled him about; and then they saw his form no more.

"But as they gazed up into heaven two men, in robes of white, appeared and said,

"You men of Galilee, why gaze you thus so anxiously upon the ascending Lord?

 Lo, he will come again from heaven as you have seen him go to heaven."[12]

1 Nicodemus, X: 18-21, *The Apocryphal New Testament Illustrated*, 76.
2 *Aquarian Gospel*, 175:12-19.
3 Ibid. 176:1-21.
4 Ibid.176: 22-31.
5 Ibid. 177:2-19.
6 Ibid. 178:1-15.
7 Ibid. 178:19-21
8 Ibid. 178:30-37; 46-47.
9 Ibid. 182:1-9
10 *Master Jesus II*.
11 "The Secret Book of James", 2, 19-35. Quoted in *The Unknown Sayings of Jesus,* 69.
12 *The Aquarian Gospel*, 180-24-26.

Epilogue

My Father, I thank Thee that Thou has given unto me
these my brethren, these fellow children. I thank Thee
that they have allowed me to enter into their
consciousness to come into the world of their creation.
I give You thanks that I might take their hand and lead
them, that I might touch them and heal them, that I
might laugh with them, and love with them, and cause
them to be as I Am, in You, forever.

Springwell, *The One*

How blessed I am to have been inspired to write this book
about Jesus the Christ. From beginning to end, this book
was written with constant and fervent prayers that only truth
would come through me to the printed page. I am reminded
of Locke's reference to seeking truth, in his *Faith and
Reason*: "He that would seriously set upon the search of
truth ought in the first place to prepare his mind with a love
of it. For he that loves it not will not take much pains to get it
nor be much concerned when he misses it. There is nobody
in the commonwealth of learning who does not profess
himself a lover of truth and There is not a rational creature
that would not take it amiss to be thought otherwise of. And
yet for all this one may truly say that there are very few
lovers of truth for truth's sake, even amongst those who
persuade themselves that they are so."[1]

The first time that Jesus came to our group (November 20,
1995), he did not identify himself. And so there are booklets
printed by Springwell Metaphysical Studies that refer to him

as *The One*. That first night we knew that it was not Archangel Gabriel channeling. It was a different kind of voice. The room was permeated with a profound peace, to the extent that we asked for a moment of silence with him that we might enjoy immersion in that peace for a time.

The reader must understand that although there was a group who attended Springwell lectures regularly and listened carefully to the wisdom imparted to us by Archangel Gabriel, we apparently did not always understand fully the lessons presented. Archangel Gabriel reminded us: "The lessons that the Master Jesus brought the last time (the seminar "The Inner Kingdom" on July 18, 1998), how many of you really understood what he was saying? You think you did? How many of you have been living the God of you completely since then? None of you. So did you get the lesson? No. You got it intellectually, but you didn't get it (p.14) . . .so you say, 'What do we do?' Very simply put, *you practice love. You consciously practice love* . . . Love of self is the creative force that takes you where you want to be and nothing else does that. Nothing else.(p.17)[2]

We are all on the journey back home to God – everyone. But each has an individual path to travel. The further removed we are from the truth of our divine being, the more we require the love and prayers of our brothers and sisters on earth. If we desire peace on earth, we must remember that it can only become a reality when we have peace in our personal lives. Going within, thanking God for our blessings, focusing on only the positive, loving ourselves as children of the Most High, are the ways in which we can know that peace profound. My journey has brought me to this book, and I recall the sweet words of Wordsworth's *Tintern Abbey*:

. . . And I have felt

A presence that disturbs me with the joy

Of elevated thoughts; a sense sublime

Of something far more deeply interfused,

Whose dwelling is the light of setting suns,

And the bound ocean and the living air,

And the blue sky, and in the mind of man:

A motion and a spirit, that impels

All thinking things, all objects of all thought,

And rolls through all things.

[1] *Historical Selections in the Philosophy of Religion*, 136.
[2] Springwell, *Illumination and Creativity*, 14 – 17.

The Master has been often referred to as the Man of Sorrows. But in his Christhood there was ever present to Him the Divine Joy.

Ferrier, *The Logia or Sayings of the Master*

BIBLIOGRAPHY

A Course in Miracles. Glen Ellen, Calif.: Foundation for Inner Peace, 1985.

The Apocryphal New Testament. London: Hone, 1820.

The Apocryphal New Testament Illustrated. Philadelphia: David McKay, 1901.

Auzou, Georges, *The Formation of the Bible*, St. Louis, Mo: B. Herder Book Co., 1963.

Barnstone, Willis, ed., *The Other Bible.* San Francisco: Harper Collins, 1984.

Bruton, David, *Baird T. Spalding – As I Knew Him.* Marina del Rey, Calif.: DeVorss, 1954.

The Christ, *New Teachings for an Awakening Humanity*, Santa Clara, Calif.: Spiritual Education Endeavors Publishing Company, 1986.

Curtis, Donald, *New Age of Understanding.* Unity Village, Mo.: Unity Books, 1973.

Dinsmore, Charles A., *The English Bible as Literature.* New York: Houghton Mifflin Co., 1931.

Emmanuel's Book, compiled by Pat Rodegast and Judith Stanton. New York: Bantam Books, 1987.

Ferrier, J. Todd, *The Logia or Sayings of the Master.* London: The Order of the Cross {1916} 1991.

Furst, Jeffrey, *Edgar Cayce's Story of Jesus*. New York: Berkley Books, 1976.

Gaer, Joseph, *What the Great Religions Believe*. New York: New American Library, 1963.

Guillaumont, A., et al., *The Gospel According to Thomas*. (In Coptic), New York: Harper & Row, 1959.

Holmes, Ernest S., *The Science of Mind*. New York: G. P. Putnam's Sons, 1984.

Holmes, Ernest S. & Fenwicke L. Holmes, *The Voice Celestial*. Los Angeles: Science of Mind Publications, 1978.

Holy Bible. King James Version.

Lamsa, George M., *Gospel Light*. San Francisco: Harper & Row, 1936.

Lamsa, George M., *Old Testament Light*. San Francisco: Harper & Row, 1964.

Lamsa, George M., *The Hidden Years of Jesus*. Lee's Summit, Mo.: Unity Books, 1968.

Larson, Martin A., *New Thought or A Modern Religious Approach*. New York: Philosophical Library, 1985.

Long, Max Freedom, *What Jesus Taught in Secret*. Marina del Rey: DeVorss & Company, 1983.

Levi, *The Aquarian Gospel of Jesus the Christ*. Marina del Rey, Calif.: DeVorss, 1907.

Manas, John H., *Divination Ancient and Modern*. New York: Pythagorean Society, 1947.

Menzies, Allan, *History of Religion*. New York: Charles Scribner's Sons, 1918.

Metaphysical Bible Dictionary. Unity Village, Mo.: Unity School of Christianity, 1931.

Meurois-Givaudan, Anne & Daniel Meurois-Givaudan, *The Way of the Essenes.* Rochester, Vt.: Destiny Books, 1993. Originally published as *De Memoire d'Essenien, l'autre visage de Jesus* (Arista Editions, Plazac, 1989).

Meyer, Marvin, *The Unknown Sayings of Jesus.* San Francisco: Harper, 1998.

Moses, Jeffrey, *Oneness.* New York: Fawcett Columbine, 1989.

Peterson, Roland, *Everyone is Right.* Marina del Rey, Calif.: DeVorss, 1986.

Potter, Charles F., *The Lost Years of Jesus Revealed.* Greenwich, Conn.: Fawcett, 1962.

Price, Ira M., *The Ancestry of Our English Bible.* New York: Harper & Brothers, 1956(1906).

Prophet, Elizabeth C., *The Lost Years of Jesus.* Livingston, Mont.: Summit University Press, 1984.

Puryear, Herbert B., *The Edgar Cayce Primer.* New York: Bantam Books, 1986.

Robinson, James M., ed., *The Nag Hammadi Library.* New York: Harper Collins, 1988.

Salz, Jeff, *Jesus in the Himalayas,* Travel Channel, April 10, 2001.

Sanderfur, Glenn, *Lives of the Master.* Virginia Beach, Va.: A.R.E. Press, 1988.

Smart, Ninian, ed., *Historical Selections in the Philosophy of Religion.* New York: Harper Row, 1962.

Smart, Ninian, *The Religious Experience of Mankind.* New York: Charles Scribner's Sons, 1969.

Spalding, Baird T., *Life and Teachings of the Masters of the Far East,* Vol. I-VI. Los Angeles: DeVorss, 1924-1955.

Springwell Metaphysical Studies. Rosendale, N.Y., 1987.
www.angelteachings.org OR gabriel@ulster.net

    Audiocassettes:
        Master Jesus I, January 18, 1997.
        Master Jesus II, May 17, 1997.
        Connecting to Your Source, November 15, 1997.
        Master Jesus III, January 17, 1998.
        The Inner Kingdom, July 18, 1998.
    Booklets:
        States of Awareness, August 6, 1994.
        Illumination and Creativity, August 7, 1994.
        The One, November 20, 1995
        The True Meaning of Christmas, December 3, 1995.
        Christ and the Antichrist, May 26, 1996.
        Recognizing Your Power, November 7, 1997
        I Am The Christ, May 1, 1998.
        The Christ Within, December 4, 1998.

Von Daniken, Erich, *Chariots of the Gods,* trans. Michael Heron, New York: G. P. Putnam's Sons, 1968.

Walsch, Neale Donald, *Conversations with God,* Vol. 1. New York: G. P. Putnam's Sons, 1996.

Wapnick, Kenneth, *Love Does Not Condemn.* Roscoe, NY: Foundation for A Course in Miracles, 1989.

Watts, Marie S., *You Are the Splendor, The Way to Spiritual Illumination.* Vista, Calif.: Marie S. Watts, 1977.

Wirt, Sherwood Eliot, *Jesus, Man of Joy.* Nashville, Tenn.: Thomas Nelson Publishers, 1991.

JESUS' JOURNEY TO THE EAST *(Possible Routes)*

It is not certain what route Jesus took on his journey to the East. Here is one possible itinerary via ancient roads and trade routes, reconstructed from the Notovitch, Abhedananda, and Roerich texts and legends. Jesus departed **Jerusalem** (follow the yellow line), took the Silk Road to **Bactra**, headed south to **Kabul**, crossed the **Punjab** and proceeded to a fair in the Kathiawar peninsula where Jain temples were later built near the town of **Palitana**. He crossed India to **Juggernaut (Puri)**, made trips to **Rajagriha (Rajgir)**, **Benares**, and other holy cities and, fleeing his enemies, went to **Kapilavastu** - birthplace of Gautama Buddha. Jesus took a trail just west of Mt. Everest to **Lhasa** (where the palace of the Dalai Lama was built in the 17th century). On the return trip (follow the violet line), he took the caravan route to **Leh**, went south to the state of **Rajputana** and then north to **Kabul**. He proceeded on the southern trade route through Persia where Zoroastrian priests abandoned him to wild beasts. Jesus survived and arrived unharmed in **Jerusalem**.

Legend:
— Jesus' journey to the East
— Jesus' return route
--- Possible alternate routes
+ Places Jesus visited according to texts and legends
a Ruins of ancient cities
≬ Passes

It is thought that Jesus passed through Ladakh on his homeward journey from Lhasa to Jerusalem.

Printed in the United States
By Bookmasters